How to Form
A
Limited
Liability
Company

HOW TO FORM

A

LIMITED

LIABILITY

COMPANY

Second Edition

Mark Warda
Attorney at Law

SPHINX® PUBLISHING
AN IMPRINT OF SOURCEBOOKS, INC.®
NAPERVILLE, ILLINOIS
www.SphinxLegal.com

Second Edition, 2003
Published by: **Sphinx® Publishing, An Imprint of Sourcebooks, Inc.®**

<u>Naperville Office</u>
P.O. Box 4410
Naperville, Illinois 60567-4410
630-961-3900
Fax: 630-961-2168
www.sourcebooks.com
www.SphinxLegal.com

This publication is designed to provide accurate and authoritative information in regard to the subject matter covered. It is sold with the understanding that the publisher is not engaged in rendering legal, accounting, or other professional service. If legal advice or other expert assistance is required, the services of a competent professional person should be sought.

From a Declaration of Principles Jointly Adopted by a Committee of the
American Bar Association and a Committee of Publishers and Associations

This product is not a substitute for legal advice.

Disclaimer required by Texas statutes.

Library of Congress Cataloging-in-Publication Data
Warda, Mark.
  How to form a limited liability company / by Mark Warda.-- 2nd ed.
      p. cm.
  Includes index.
  ISBN 1-57248-222-2 (pbk. : alk. paper)
  1. Private companies--United States--Popular works. 2. Limited
partnership--United States--Popular works. I. Title.
KF1380.Z9W37 2003
346.73'0668--dc21
                              2002155733

CONTENTS

USING SELF-HELP LAW BOOKS

Before using a self-help law book, you should realize the advantages and disadvantages of doing your own legal work and understand the challenges and diligence that this requires.

THE GROWING TREND

Rest assured that you won't be the first or only person handling your own legal matter. For example, in some states, more than seventy-five percent of divorces and other cases have at least one party representing him or herself. Because of the high cost of legal services, this is a major trend and many courts are struggling to make it easier for people to represent themselves. However, some courts are not happy with people who do not use attorneys and refuse to help them in any way. For some, the attitude is, "Go to the law library and figure it out for yourself."

We at Sphinx write and publish self-help law books to give people an alternative to the often complicated and confusing legal books found in most law libraries. We have made the explanations of the law as simple and easy to understand as possible. Of course, unlike an attorney advising an individual client, we cannot cover every conceivable possibility.

COST/VALUE ANALYSIS

Whenever you shop for a product or service, you are faced with various levels of quality and price. In deciding what product or service to buy, you make a cost/value analysis on the basis of your willingness to pay and the quality you desire.

When buying a car, you decide whether you want transportation, comfort, status, or sex appeal. Accordingly, you decide among such choices as a Neon, a Lincoln, a Rolls Royce, or a Porsche. Before making a decision, you usually weigh the merits of each option against the cost.

When you get a headache, you can take a pain reliever (such as aspirin) or visit a medical specialist for a neurological examination. Given this choice, most people, of course, take a pain reliever, since it costs only pennies; whereas a medical examination costs hundreds of dollars and takes a lot of time. This is usually a logical choice because it is rare to need anything more than a pain reliever for a headache. But in some cases, a headache may indicate a brain tumor and failing to see a specialist right away can result in complications. Should everyone with a headache go to a specialist? Of course not, but people treating their own illnesses must realize that they are betting on the basis of their cost/value analysis of the situation. They are taking the most logical option.

The same cost/value analysis must be made when deciding to do one's own legal work. Many legal situations are very straight forward, requiring a simple form and no complicated analysis. Anyone with a little intelligence and a book of instructions can handle the matter without outside help.

But there is always the chance that complications are involved that only an attorney would notice. To simplify the law into a book like this, several legal cases often must be condensed into a single sentence or paragraph. Otherwise, the book would be several hundred pages long and too complicated for most people. However, this simplification necessarily leaves out many details and nuances that would apply to special or unusual situations. Also, there are many ways to interpret most legal questions. Your case may come before a judge who disagrees with the analysis of our authors.

Therefore, in deciding to use a self-help law book and to do your own legal work, you must realize that you are making a cost/value analysis. You have decided that the money you will save in doing it yourself outweighs the chance that your case will not turn out to your satisfaction. Most people handling their own simple legal matters never have a problem, but occasionally people find that it ended up costing them more to have an attorney straighten out the situation than it would have if they had hired an attorney in the beginning. Keep this in mind if you decide to handle your own case, and be sure to consult an attorney if you feel you might need further guidance.

LOCAL RULES   The next thing to remember is that a book that covers the law for the entire nation, or even for an entire state, cannot possibly include every procedural difference of every county court. Whenever possible, we provide the exact form needed; however, in some areas, each county, or even each judge, may require unique forms and procedures. In our *state* books, our forms usually cover the majority of counties in the state, or provide examples of the type of form that will be required. In our *national* books, our forms are sometimes even more general in nature but are designed to give a good idea of the type of form that will be needed in most locations. Nonetheless, keep in mind that your *state*, county, or judge may have a requirement, or use a form, that is not included in this book.

You should not necessarily expect to be able to get all of the information and resources you need solely from within the pages of this book. This book will serve as your guide, giving you specific information whenever possible and helping you to find out what else you will need to know. This is just like if you decided to build your own backyard deck. You might purchase a book on how to build decks. However, such a book would not include the building codes and permit requirements of every city, town, county, and township in the nation; nor would it include the lumber, nails, saws, hammers, and other materials and tools you would need to actually build the deck. You would use the book as your guide, and then do some work and research involving such matters as whether you need a permit of some kind, what type and grade of wood are available in your area, whether to use hand tools or power tools, and how to use those tools.

Before using the forms in a book like this, you should check with your court clerk to see if there are any local rules of which you should be aware, or local forms you will need to use. Often, such forms will require the same information as the forms in the book but are merely laid out differently, use slightly different language, or use different color paper so the clerks can easily find them. They will sometimes require additional information.

CHANGES IN
THE LAW

Besides being subject to state and local rules and practices, the law is subject to change at any time. The courts and the legislatures of all fifty states are constantly revising the laws. It is possible that while you are reading this book, some aspect of the law is being changed or a court is interpreting a law in a different way. You should always check the most recent statutes, rules and regulations to see what, if any changes have been made.

In most cases, the change will be of minimal significance. A form will be redesigned, additional information will be required, or a waiting period will be extended. As a result, you might need to revise a form, file an extra form, or wait out a longer time period; these types of changes will not usually affect the outcome of your case. On the other hand, sometimes a major part of the law is changed, the entire law in a particular area is rewritten, or a case that was the basis of a central legal point is overruled. In such instances, your entire ability to pursue your case may be impaired.

Again, you should weigh the value of your case against the cost of an attorney and make a decision as to what you believe is in your best interest.

INTRODUCTION

Each year millions of new businesses are registered throughout the country. For years *corporations* have been the preferred form of business, but the *limited liability company* is becoming more popular each year. The reason for this is that limited liability companies provide more flexibility and less paperwork than corporations, while offering nearly identical benefits.

The main reason people incorporate or form limited liability companies is to avoid personal liability for business debts and liabilities. While sole proprietors and partners are at risk of losing nearly everything they own, entrepreneurs who form an LLC or corporation risk only the *capital* they put up to start the venture. For this reason, the limited liability company is one of the few inexpensive protections left.

Before you start an LLC, you should review the advantages and disadvantages and the types of LLCs available. In most cases, an LLC will be better for you than other types of businesses, but in some cases it may be more expensive or have other disadvantages. These matters are explained in Chapters 1, 2 and 3.

Creating a basic limited liability company is not difficult and it is the purpose of this book to explain, in simple language, how you can do it yourself. In most states you can form your own LLC using just the forms in this book. However, in some states, special state forms may be required. These requirements have changed frequently over the years. As explained in Chapter 4, it is best to obtain your state's latest LLC formation materials before registering your LLC. Some states provide only a short instruction sheet with no forms, but others have optional or required forms.

One document that no state provides is the *operating agreeement* for the LLC. This is an important document and is explained in Chapter 4. Two different operating agreements are contained in Appendix C, depending on whether your LLC will be managed by the members or by managers.

The fifty states have not all passed the same LLC law. Each one had it's own committee review the proposed law, which was subject to amendments by legislators. Therefore, a book of this kind cannot give you an exact answer to the fine details of your state's laws.

However, it can give you the general principles that apply to LLCs. Appendix A includes summaries of the main points of each state's laws. For more details, you should obtain a copy of your state's LLC statute and the formation materials provided by your secretary of state. In fact, because the statutes are amended so often, you should check the statute before filing your papers.

Some states provide free copies of the LLC statute through the secretary of state's office or through the state legislators' offices. If your state does not do this, you can photocopy the law at the library. A law library would probably have a more up-to-date statute than a public library.

Most states also have their statutes available on the Internet. You can access state laws from any of these sites:

www.findlaw.com/11stategov/index.html

www.law.cornell.edu/states/listing.html

www.alllaw.com/StatMeg.html

The limited liability company you form can be managed by the members or it can delegate management powers to managers who are or are not members. Whenever management is delegated to managers you should be aware of securities laws. This is explained in Chapter 5.

Chapters 6, 7, and 8 discuss the day-to-day activities of an LLC. In addition, they include explanations of raising capital, amending the original agreement, and dissolving an LLC.

A Glossary of legal terms and a section called "For Further Reference" give additional information to the reader. Appendix A lists relevant statutes—state-by-state. Appendix B contains sample filled-in forms and Appendix C offers blank, perforated forms for the reader to use.

If your situation is in any way complicated or involves factors not mentioned in this book, you should seek the advice of an attorney practicing business law. The cost of a short consultation can be a lot cheaper than the consequences of violating the law. Keep in mind, however, that the limited liability company is a special entity and few attorneys have much experience with them. The best attorney in this type of situation is one who promotes himself or herself as practicing in this area.

This book also explains the basics of taxation, but you should discuss your own particular situation with your accountant before deciding what is best for you. He or she can also set you up with an efficient system of bookkeeping that can save both time and money.

Good luck with your new business!

WHAT A LIMITED LIABILITY COMPANY IS

1

A *limited liability company* is a relatively recent "invention." For hundreds of years, the three choices of entity were *sole proprietorship*, *partnership*, or *corporation*; but in 1977 the LLC was invented by the state of Wyoming to fill a new need–businesses that wanted to be taxed and managed like partnerships but protected from liability like a corporation. Once the IRS accepted this arrangement, every state in the union followed suit and passed a law allowing LLCs.

The laws, however, were not identical and the effectiveness of the LLCs varied from state to state. In the beginning, single-person businesses could not use them because the law stated that a sole person could not be taxed as a partnership. But in 1997, the IRS changed the law to allow single-person LLCs to pass through their income to the owner.

Because the early tax laws required two or more members to avoid corporate taxation, many state laws required two persons to start an LLC. But after the tax law change, all fifty states now allow one member LLCs.

In some states there are disadvantages to using LLCs because the filing fees or annual fees are higher than for other types of businesses, such as an *S* corporation. Before forming your own LLC, you should compare the fees and requirements to be sure it offers your business the most advantages.

Legally, an LLC is a legal *person*, like a corporation, that is created under state law. As a person, an LLC has certain rights and obligations, such as the right to do business and the obligation to pay taxes. (Sometimes one hears of a law referring to *natural persons*. That is to differentiate natural persons from corporations and LLCs, which, stated earlier, are considered persons, but not natural persons.)

LIMITED PERSONAL RISK
The idea behind both the LLC and the corporation is to allow people to invest in a new business but not risk unlimited personal liability. Before the corporation was invented hundreds of years ago, people who invested in, say, an expedition to the New World to look for gold, could lose everything they owned in the event the venture went into debt. The invention of the corporation allowed people to put a limited sum of money into such a venture, split the profits if it succeeded, and not be liable for more if it failed.

The reasons for having a corporation or LLC are the same today. They allow investors to put up money for new ventures without risk of further liability. However, before forming an LLC, you should be familiar with the following common terms that will be used in the text.

MEMBER
A *member* is a person who owns an interest in a limited liability company. It is similar to the stockholder of a corporation. In an LLC the members have the option of running the company themselves or having managers who are or are not members. Until recently, some states required an LLC to have two or more members, but now that the IRS allows favorable tax treatment for one-member LLCs, the states are changing their laws to allow them.

MANAGER
A *manager* is someone who runs the affairs of an LLC. In most states an LLC can be either managed by all the members equally, or it can have a manager or managers who may or may not be members.

REGISTERED AGENT AND REGISTERED OFFICE

The *registered agent* is the person designated by a limited liability company to receive legal papers that must be served on the company. (In a few states the term *statutory agent* is used.) The registered agent should be regularly available at the registered office of the corporation. The *registered office* can be the company offices or the office of the company's attorney or whomever is the registered agent. At the time of registration, some states require the company to file a Certificate of Designation of Registered Agent/Registered Office. This contains a statement that must be signed by the registered agent that he or she understands the duties and responsibilities of the position.

ARTICLES OF ORGANIZATION

Articles of Organization is the document that is filed to start the limited liability company. (In a few states, it may have a slightly different name, such as *certificate of organization*.) In most cases it legally needs to contain only a few basic statements. More provisions can be added, but usually it is better to put such provisions in the membership agreement rather than the articles because amendment of the latter is more complicated.

OPERATING AGREEMENT

The *operating agreement* is the document that sets out rights and obligations of the members and the rules for running the company. An operating agreement is not required in every state, but having one is a good idea. If such an agreement has not been signed by the members, the rules provided in your state's statutes apply.

MEMBERSHIP OPERATING AGREEMENT

If the LLC is run by its members, the agreement is usually called a *membership operating agreement*. Even if the LLC has only one member, it is important to have an operating agreement to spell out the fact of nonliability of the member for debts of the company.

MANAGEMENT OPERATING AGREEMENT

If the LLC is to be managed by less than all the members, or by someone who is not a member, there should be a management agreement spelling out the rights and duties of the members and the managers. This can be combined into the operating agreement, in which case it would be called a *management operating agreement*.

ANNUAL
REPORT

Most states require some sort of annual report to keep the state updated on the members and status of the company. In most cases, the company will be dissolved if this form is not filed on time and in some states there is a very high fee to reinstate the company.

OTHER
FORMS

Some states require various other forms to establish an LLC. These will be mentioned in Appendix A or in materials you may receive from your state.

ADVANTAGES AND DISADVANTAGES OF AN LLC

2

Before forming a limited liability company, the business owner or prospective business owner should become familiar with the advantages and disadvantages of the LLC and how they compare to those of other business entities.

COMPARED TO PROPRIETORSHIPS AND PARTNERSHIPS

The limited liability company offers the greatest benefits when compared to partnerships and *sole proprietorships*. Now that the LLC structure is available, it is advisable for most partnerships and sole proprietorships to switch.

ADVANTAGES
Limited liability. The main reason for forming a limited liability company or corporation is to limit the liability of the owners. In a sole proprietorship or partnership, the owners are personally liable for the debts and liabilities of the business, and creditors can go after nearly all of their assets to collect. If an LLC is formed and operated properly, the owners can be protected from all such liability.

Example 1: If several people are in a partnership and one of them makes many large extravagant purchases in the name of the partnership, the other partners can be liable for the full amount of all such purchases. The creditors can take the bank accounts, cars, real estate, and other property of any partner to pay the debts of the partnership. If only one partner has money, he or she may have to pay all of the debts accumulated by the other partners. When doing business in the LLC or corporate form, the business may go bankrupt and the shareholders may lose their initial investment, but the creditors cannot touch the personal assets of the owners.

Example 2: If an employee of a partnership causes a terrible accident, such as in a car crash in which someone is paralyzed, the partnership and all of the partners can be held personally liable for millions of dollars in damages. With a corporation or LLC, only the business would be liable whether or not there was enough money to cover the damages.

One true example of this is a business owner who owned hundreds of taxis. He put one or two in each of hundreds of different corporations that he owned. Each corporation only had minimum insurance and when one taxi was involved in an accident, the owner only lost the assets of that corporation. The injured party tried to reach the owner's other assets, but the court ruled that this was a valid use of the corporate structure.

NOTE: *If a member of a limited liability company does something negligent himself, signs a debt personally, or guarantees a company debt, the limited liability company will not protect him from the consequences of his own act or from the debt. Also, if a limited liability company fails to follow some formality, a court may use that as an excuse to hold the members liable. The formalities include having separate bank accounts, filing annual reports, and following other requirements of state law.*

Since the limited liability company is relatively new, there have been few cases interpreting the law. Courts will most likely look to both corporation and partnership law when ruling in a limited liability company case. When a court ignores a corporate structure and holds the owners or officers liable, it is called *piercing the corporate veil.* (It is not yet clear how or when the courts would allow a party to pierce the LLC structure.)

Continuous existence. A limited liability company may have a *perpetual existence.* When a sole proprietor dies, the assets of his or her business may pass to the heirs but the business does not exist any longer. (This may also happen with a partnership if it is not set up right.) If the surviving spouse or other heirs of a business owner want to continue the business in their own names, they will be considered a new business even if they are using the assets of the old business. With a partnership, the death of one partner can cause a dissolution of the business if there is no provision in the partnership agreement for it to continue.

Example: If the owner of a sole proprietorship dies, his or her spouse may want to continue the business. That person may inherit all of the assets but would have to start a new business. This means getting new licenses and tax numbers, registering the name, and establishing credit from scratch. With an LLC, the business continues with all of the same licenses, bank accounts, etc.

Ease of transferability. A limited liability company, and all of its assets and accounts, may be transferred by the simple transfer of interest in the company. With a sole proprietorship, each of the individual assets must be transferred and the accounts, licenses, and permits must be individually transferred.

Example: If a sole proprietorship is sold, the new owner will have to get a new occupational license, set up his or her own bank account, and apply for a new taxpayer identification number. The title to any vehicles or real estate will have to be put in his name, and all open accounts will have to be changed to his name. He will probably have to submit new credit applications. With an LLC or corporation, all of these items remain in the same business name and are under control of the new manager or officer.

NOTE: *In some cases, the new owners will have to submit personal applications for such things as credit lines or liquor licenses.*

Sharing ownership. With a limited liability company, the owner of a business can share the profits of a business without giving up control. This is done by setting up the shares of profits different from the shares of ownership in the membership agreement.

Example: John wants to give his children some of the profits of his business. He can make them members of the company entitled to a share of the profits without giving them any control over the management. This would not be practical with a partnership or sole proprietorship.

Ease of raising capital. A limited liability company may raise capital by admitting new members or borrowing money. In most cases, a business does not pay taxes on money it raises through the sale of its shares.

Example: If an LLC or corporation wants to expand, the owners can sell ten percent, fifty percent, or ninety percent of the ownership and still remain in control of the business. The people putting up the money may be more willing to invest if they know they will have a piece of the action than if they were making a loan with a limited return. They may not want to become partners in a partnership.

NOTE: *There are strict rules about selling interests in businesses with criminal penalties and triple damages for violators. See Chapter 5.*

Separate record keeping. An LLC has all its own bank accounts and records. A sole proprietor may have trouble differentiating which expenses were for business and which were for personal items.

Ease of estate planning. With an LLC or corporation, shares of a company can be distributed more easily than with a partnership or sole proprietorship. Different heirs can be given different percentages and control can be limited to those who are most capable.

Prestige. The name of an LLC or corporation sounds more prestigious than the name of a sole proprietor to some people. John Smith d/b/a Acme Builders sounds like one lone guy. Acme Builders, L.L.C., sounds like it might be a large sophisticated operation. One female writer on the subject has suggested that a woman who is president of a corporation looks more successful than one doing business in her own name. This would be the same with an LLC and probably would apply to everyone.

Separate credit rating. An LLC has its own credit rating, which can be better or worse than the owner's credit rating. An LLC can go bankrupt while the owner's credit remains unaffected, or an owner's credit may be bad, but the corporation may maintain a good rating.

DISADVANTAGES   ***Cost.*** Compared to a sole proprietorship or partnership, an LLC is more expensive to operate. In some states the fees are as low as $50 or even $10, but in others they are hundreds of dollars each year. However, this cost is offset by the lesser need for liability insurance.

Separate records. The owners of a limited liability company must be careful to keep their personal business separate from the business of the limited liability company. The limited liability company must have its own records and should have minutes of meetings. Money must be kept separate. However, in every business records should be separate, so the company structure might make this easier.

Taxes. A limited liability company owner will have to pay *unemployment compensation tax* for himself, which he would not have to pay as a sole proprietor.

Banking. Checks made out to a limited liability company cannot be cashed; they must be deposited into a corporate account. Some banks have higher fees just for businesses that are incorporated. See pages 34–35 for tips on avoiding high bank fees.

COMPARED TO LIMITED PARTNERSHIPS

A limited partnership is an entity in which one or more partners control the business and are liable for the debts (the general partners) and one or more partners have no say in the business nor liability for the debts (the limited partners). This is expensive to set up because the limited partnership agreement is costly.

The limited liability company allows a similar structure at a lower cost with the added benefit that no one needs to be liable for the debts of the business. For most businesses that were once limited partnerships, the LLC is now the preferred form of business.

COMPARED TO CORPORATIONS

ADVANTAGES

For a small business, there is not a great difference between an LLC and an S corporation. The main differences between an LLC and a corporation are the following points.

- An LLC requires less formality than a corporation. While improper procedures in a corporation may allow a creditor to *pierce the corporate veil* and hold shareholders liable, the LLC is meant to be a safe harbor to protect business owners from liability.

- An LLC can make special allocations of profits and losses among members; whereas an S corporation cannot. S corporations must have one class of ownership in which profits and losses are allocated according to the percentage of ownership.

- In an LLC, money borrowed by the company can increase the *tax basis* of the owners (and lower the taxes); whereas in an S corporation, it does not.

- Contributing property to set up an LLC is not taxable even for minority interest owners. In the case of a corporation, the Internal Revenue Code Section 351 only allows it to be tax free for the contributors who have control of the business.

- The owners of an LLC can be foreign persons, other corporations or any kind of trust. This is not true for the owners of S corporations.

- An LLC may have an unlimited number of members while an S corporation is limited to seventy-five.

- If an S corporation violates one of the rules, it can lose its S corporation status and not be allowed to regain it for five years.

- In some states an LLC enjoys double asset protection. While a corporation protects shareholders from claims against a corporation, some states protect an LLC from claims against its members. If an LLC has two or more members, then a claim against just one member cannot affect the business of the LLC.

NOTE: *Another advantage may be psychological. The LLC is still a relatively new entity, and in the twenty-first century it may look more up-to-date to be an LLC rather than an ordinary corporation.*

DISADVANTAGES
The main disadvantage of an LLC compared to an S corporation is that with an S corporation, profits taken out other than salary are not subject to social security and medicare taxes (15.3% at the time of publication); whereas all profits of an LLC are subject to these taxes (up to the taxable limits).

For a large business where the owners take out salaries of $80,000 or more plus profits, there would not be much difference since the social security tax cuts out at about that level. But for a smaller business where an owner would take out, say, $30,000 salary and $20,000 profit, the extra taxes would be over $3,000.

In some states, a disadvantage of an LLC is that its start-up fee, or annual fees, are higher than for an S corporation.

CONVERTING AN EXISTING BUSINESS

While an LLC may appear to be the best type of business entity for you, if you have an existing business you should weigh the time and expense involved in making the conversion.

A sole proprietorship would be the easiest to convert and a corporation would be the most complicated. (The corporation has potential tax issues which should be reviewed by a tax specialist.) At a minimum, some of the things which will have to be handled in your conversion are federal employer identification number, state tax account numbers, fictitious name registration, business licenses, professional licenses (if any), bank accounts, vendor accounts, customer accounts, and utilities.

Business Comparison Chart

	Sole Proprietorship	General Partnership	Limited Partnership	Limited Liability Co.	Corporation C or S	Nonprofit Corporation
Liability Protection	No	No	For limited partners	For all members	For all shareholders	For all members
Taxes	Pass through	Pass through	Pass through	Pass through or LLC can pay	S corps. pass through C corps. pay tax	None on income– Employees pay on wages
Minimum # of members	1	2	2	1	1	1 to 3
Diff. classes of ownership	No	Yes	Yes	Yes	S corps. No C corps. Yes	No ownership Different classes of membership
Survives after Death	No	No	Yes	Yes	Yes	Yes
Best for	1 person low-risk business or no assets	low-risk business	low-risk business with silent partners	All types of businesses	All types of businesses	Educational

Types of LLCs 3

Domestic LLC or Foreign LLC

A person wishing to form a limited liability company must decide whether the company will be a *domestic* LLC or a *foreign* LLC. For our purposes, a domestic LLC is one you form in the state in which you do business, and a foreign LLC is one you form in another state to do business in your state.

DELAWARE LLCs
In the past, there was an advantage to forming a business in Delaware, because of its liberal business laws and a long history of court decisions favorable to businesses. Many national corporations were formed there for that reason. However, most states have liberalized their business laws over the years. Today, in most cases, there is no advantage to forming a business in Delaware unless you are doing business there.

NEVADA LLCs
Nevada has liberalized its business laws recently to attract more companies. It allows more privacy and other benefits depending on the type of entity. It does not have a state income tax, nor does it share information with the Internal Revenue Service. If you are concerned about privacy, you should review the Nevada information page in Appendix A and compare the costs to those in your own state.

DISADVANTAGE The biggest disadvantage to forming a business in Nevada, Delaware, or any state other than the one you are in, is that you will need to have an agent or an office in that state and will have to register as a foreign corporation doing business in your state. This is more expensive and more complicated than registering in your own state. You can also be sued in the state in which your company was formed. This would be more expensive for you to defend than a suit filed in your local court. Additionally, if you incorporate in a state which has an income tax, you may have to pay taxes there even if you only do business in your own state.

MEMBERSHIP CONTROLLED OR MANAGEMENT CONTROLLED

The next thing you will need to decide is whether your LLC will be membership controlled or management controlled. If the LLC is being formed by one person or a small group of people who will all operate it as partners, you should designate it as membership controlled and execute a *membership operating agreement*. If the LLC will have silent partners and be managed by other members or nonmembers, you should designate it management controlled and execute a *management operating agreement*. These documents are explained in the next chapter and are included in Appendix C.

LLC OR PLLC

In many states, professionals such as lawyers, doctors, veterinarians, architects, life insurance agents, chiropractors, and accountants are allowed to set up LLCs. These are designated *PLLCs* or something of a similar nature.

Again, since the laws covering professional LLCs are state laws, you will need to get a copy of your state's statute to be sure your plan complies with all of the requirements. You should also check with the *licensing board* that regulates your profession to see if they impose any additional requirements on professional LLCs. In some states, professionals may be required to obtain malpractice insurance if they form a PLLC.

Following are some of the other types of rules that may apply to professional LLCs.

- The professional limited liability company must have one specific purpose spelled out in the articles of organization and the purpose must be to practice one of the professions. Usually the PLLC may not engage in any other business, but it may invest its funds in real estate, stocks, bonds, mortgages, or other types of investments.

- The name of the professional service corporation must contain the word "chartered" or "professional limited company" or the abbreviation "PLLC."

- Only persons licensed to practice the profession may be members of a professional service limited liability company, and a member who loses his or her right to practice must immediately sever all employment with and financial interests in the company.

- A professional service limited liability company may not merge with any other limited liability company except another professional service corporation that is licensed to perform the same type of services.

Start-Up Procedures 4

Choosing the Company Name

The very first thing to do before starting a limited liability company is to thoroughly check out the name you wish to use to be sure it is available. Many businesses have been forced to stop using their name after spending thousands of dollars promoting it.

LOCAL
RECORDS

To check for other businesses in your state using a certain name, you can call or write your secretary of state's office, or in some states you can do your own search using their web site. The phone number, address and web site address for your state (if any) is on the state page in Appendix A. If your name is too similar to another company's name, you will not be allowed to register it.

You should also ask about *fictitious* or *assumed names*. In some states, these are registered with the secretary of state and in others, with the county recorder or court office. In some states, the secretary of state does not limit the number of people who may register the same name. Whether there was infringement would depend upon whether they used the name in the same area.

BUSINESS
LISTINGS

Since some businesses neglect to properly register their name (yet still may have superior rights to the name), you should also check phone books and business directories. Many libraries have phone books from around the country as well as directories of trade names.

YELLOW PAGE
LISTINGS

If you have Internet access, you can search every yellow pages listing for free. Just search for "yellow pages" with any web search engine (i.e., Yahoo, WebCrawler, Lycos, etc.). You can select a state, enter your business name and it will tell you if any other companies are listed with that name. One site that allows you to search all states at once is:

www.switchboard.com

Since the sites may not be 100% accurate, you should check a few different ones to be sure your search is thorough. If you do not have access to a computer, you may be able to use one at your public library or have the search done for you at the library for a small fee.

TRADEMARK
SEARCH

To be sure that your use of the name does not violate someone else's trademark rights, you should have a trademark search done of the mark in the United States Patent and Trademark Office. In the past, this required a visit to their offices or the hiring of a search firm for over a hundred dollars. But in 1999, the USPTO put its trademark records online and you can now search them at: **www.uspto.gov** by clicking on the "Search" link.

If you do not have access to the Internet, you can contact your local library or one of the firms listed below. Some firms that do searches are:

Government Liaison Services, Inc.
200 North Glebe Rd., Suite 321
P.O. Box 3292
Arlington, VA 22203
(800) 642-6564, (703) 524-8200
Fax: (703) 525-8451
www.trademarkinfo.com

Thomson & Thomson
500 Victory Road
North Quincy, MA 02171-3145
800-692-8833
Fax: (617) 479-5398
www.thomson-thomson.com

XL Corporate Service
62 White Street
New York, NY 10013
800-221-2972

SIMILAR
NAMES

Sometimes it seems like every good name is taken. But a name can often be modified slightly or used for a different type of goods or services. If there is a "TriCounty Painting, L.L.C." in another part of your state, it may be possible to use something like "TriCounty Painting of Libertyville, L.L.C." if you are in a different part of the state. Try different variations if your favorite is taken. Keep in mind that if you eventually expand your business to an area where the name is being used, you can be barred from using it in that area. In such a case, you would be better off using a completely different name.

Another possibility is to give the corporation one name and do business under a fictitious name. (See FICTITIOUS OR ASSUMED NAMES on page 24.)

Example: If you want to use the name "Flowers by Freida" in your city and there is already a "Flowers by Freida, Inc." in another part of the state, you might register your company under the name "Freida Jones, L.L.C." and register the company as doing business under the fictitious name "Flowers by Freida." Unless "Flowers by Freida, Inc." has registered a state or federal trademark for the name, you will probably be able to use the name.

NOTE: *You should realize that you might run into complications later, especially if you decide to expand into other areas of the state. One protection available would be to register the name as a trademark. This would give you exclusive use of the name anywhere that someone else was not already using it. (See page 23.)*

NAME
REQUIREMENTS

There are requirements that the limited liability company name contain wording indicating that it is a limited liability company. Depending on the state, it may require one or all of the following:

L.C.	LC	limited company
L.L.C.	LLC	limited liability company

In some states you can use just the word "limited" or the abbreviation "ltd.," but in others, you cannot. Be sure to check your state rules before making a choice.

The name cannot include any words implying that it is part of the state or federal government or that it is in any business in which it is not authorized to be.

In some states, professional LLCs must also use certain words, such as "chartered" or "professional limited liability company." Again, the specific state rule must be checked.

FORBIDDEN
NAMES

A limited liability company may not use certain words in its name if there would be a likelihood of confusion. There are state and federal laws that control the use of these words. In most cases, your application will be rejected if you use a forbidden word. Some of the words that may not be used in some states without special licenses or registration are:

Assurance	Insurance
Banc	Lottery
Bank	Olympiad
Banker	Olympic
Banking	Savings Bank
College	Savings and Loan Association
Cooperative	Spaceport Florida
Credit Union	Trust Company
Disney	University
Florida Spaceport	

TRADEMARKS The name of a business cannot be registered as a trademark, but if the name is used in connection with goods or services, it may be registered and such registration will grant the holder exclusive rights to use that name except in areas where someone else has already used the name. A trademark may be registered either in each state or in the United States Patent and Trademark Office which covers the entire country.

Each trademark is registered for a certain "class" of goods. If you want to sell "Zapata" chewing gum, it doesn't matter that someone has registered the name "Zapata" for use in another category, such as shoes. (An exception to this rule is where a trademark has become famous. For example, even though Coca-Cola is a trademark for a beverage, you could not use the name Coca-Cola for chewing gum.) If you want to register the mark for several types of goods or services, you must register it for each different class into which the goods or services fall, and pay a separate fee for each category.

Every state has a procedure for registering a trademark for statewide protection. This protects a mark throughout the state from anyone who might want to use the same mark in the future, but does not affect the rights of people who have already been using the mark in the state. It also does not stop people in other states from using the mark. The form is simple and the cost is minimal in most states. For more information, phone, write or check the web site of your secretary of state.

For protection across the entire United States, the mark can be registered with the United States Patent and Trademark Office for a fee of $325. The procedure for federal registration is more complicated than state registration. You can find some information and forms on the website of the United States Patent and Trademark Office:

www.uspto.gov

FICTITIOUS OR ASSUMED NAMES

The name of an LLC is its legal name. However, it can also operate under a *fictitious name* (called an *assumed name* in some states) just as an individual can. This is done when a company wants to operate several businesses under different names or if the business name is not available as a company name.

Example: An LLC may have the legal name Elizabeth Bartlett, LLC, and open a bakery called Betty B's Breads & Buns.

Registration of a fictitious name is either done with the secretary of state or a county recorder. Check with the office in your area for forms and instructions.

NOTE: *When a fictitious name is used by a limited liability company, the company's legal name should also be used in conjunction with it whenever possible. If the public does not see that they are dealing with a limited liability company, they may be able to use the same theory of* piercing the corporate veil *to collect against the members individually.*

STATE LLC LAWS AND FORMS

Each state has adopted its own version of the statute allowing LLCs, so each state will have slightly different requirements as to what the filing documents must contain. Also, not every state will supply the same materials. Some send only a single page of vague instructions, others send a large packet including a copy of the statute and numerous forms.

If your state provides a form, it may speed up your processing if you use that form. Some states provide the form in downloadable format on the Internet, but others only use the mail. If you have access to the Internet, you can check the site for your state listed in Appendix A.

California appears to be the only state which requires that its own form be used. Others allow people to draft their own articles as long as all the required information is included. The California form is included in Appendix C.

If your state does not provide a form, or if you wish to get started without waiting for the form, you can use the blank form in this book or retype the information yourself. The good thing about forming an LLC is that if you make a mistake, such as forgetting a required provision, the filing office will usually return it for correction rather than let you file it wrong and have a defective company.

One form which no state supplies is the operating agreement. This is explained later in this chapter and blank forms are included in Appendix C.

Summaries of the state *statutes* are included in Appendix A, but because the laws are new, they are being fine tuned every year or two. Your state's laws may have changed by the time you read this. You can get the statutes for most states on the Internet. (See the Introduction to this book for sites.) If you do not have access to the Internet, you may be able to obtain a copy from your secretary of state or your state legislator, or photocopy it at the library.

When getting a copy of your state statute, find out the date it was last updated and when your state legislature convenes. If a session recently ended, there may be changes to the law that are not included in the statute you have. A librarian at a law library would be most knowledgeable as to which copy of the statute is most up-to-date.

Once you get a copy of the laws, you should become familiar with the filing and operational requirements for LLCs. General rules are included in this book, but some states have some more specific requirements. Don't be intimidated if the statute is long. Many of the provisions will apply to *mergers* or *dissolutions*, which do not concern you at this point.

ARTICLES OF ORGANIZATION

The action that creates the limited liability company in most states is the filing of articles of organization with the secretary of state. In a few states there may be another filing office or the document may have a slightly different name. Some states require additional forms to complete the registration as explained on page 29.

USUAL
REQUIREMENTS

Requirements for the articles of organization are listed below. Some states require an extra clause or two, which is discussed in the next section.

Name. Must include the suffix (LLC, LC, etc.).

Purpose. Many states require that the business purpose be stated, though this may be stated as "any lawful purpose for which limited liability companies may be formed." A few states ask for a specific *industry code.*

Period of duration. This may be stated as perpetual in most states. In Utah, it cannot exceed ninety-nine years, and in Nebraska and South Dakota, it cannot exceed thirty years.

Name and street address of the initial registered (or statutory) agent. In many states, the registered agent also must sign a form stating that he or she is familiar with and accepts the obligations of the position.

Each limited liability company must have a *registered agent* and a *registered office.* The registered agent can be any individual or a corporation. The registered office can be the business office of the limited liability company if the registered agent works out of that office, or it can be the office of another individual who is the registered agent (such as an attorney) or a corporate registered agent's office. The business address of the registered agent is considered the registered office of the limited liability company. In most LLCs, one of the members is the registered agent at the business address. Technically, it may not be a residence unless that address is also a business office of the limited liability company.

Management. Must state whether the company will be managed by the members or by separate managers. In most states, all of their names and addresses must be included, whether or not they are members or separate managers.

Principle place of business. This must be a street addresses in most states, but a mailing address can also be included.

Effective date. Many states want to know the effective date of the articles. Usually, this is the date of filing.

Nonliability. Five states (Hawaii, South Carolina, South Dakota, Vermont, and West Virginia) require a statement of whether the members are liable for the debts of the company. Several other states say that a clause can be added stating whether the members are liable. Since the main purpose of forming an LLC is to avoid personal liability, we have included a nonliability clause in the articles in this book. If using a state form, you should not check any box stating that the members are liable.

It is best to keep your articles to the bare legal minimum and put any other *provisions* in the operating agreement. This is because it is much easier to amend the operating agreement than the articles if you want to make changes at a later date.

ADDITIONAL CLAUSES

The following clauses are sometimes put into LLC articles. In some states, one or more of these clauses may be required. See your state page in Appendix A for "Articles Special Requirements."

The right, if any, to admit new members. If the LLC will allow new members to be admitted, there must be a clause stating so. Some states require this to be in the articles along with the terms and conditions of admission. Here is some sample language:

```
New members can be admitted to the company with full
rights of membership upon the unanimous consent of the
existing members.
```

Members' Rights to Continue Business. This clause states whether the remaining members can continue the business after the death, retirement, resignation, expulsion, bankruptcy, dissolution of a member or any other event that terminates membership. Some states require that this be spelled out. Here is a sample clause:

```
The company can continue the business after the death,
retirement, resignation, expulsion, bankruptcy, disso-
lution of a member or any other event that terminates
membership, upon the unanimous consent of the
remaining members.
```

Organizers. In some cases, the organizers of the company are different from the members (such as if an attorney or paralegal files the papers). Colorado, the District of Columbia, Illinois, and Oregon require that the organizers be disclosed in the articles.

PROFESSIONAL
LLCs

In most states there is a whole separate portion of the statutes that govern "professional LLCs" and other professional companies. This contains specific requirements that these entities must follow. Some typical things that the statute may require are:

- the business purpose is limited to the practice of the one profession for which it was organized;

- no person or entity can be admitted as a member unless he, she, or it is qualified to practice the profession and no interest can be sold except to someone so qualified; and,

- some states require members of professional LLCs to carry certain limits of malpractice insurance.

If forming a professional LLC, you should obtain a copy of the statute that governs them in your state. Also, check with the board that regulates your profession–they may have additional regulations that apply. If they do not provide a form, you can use the form included in this book, adding the necessary clauses to "Article IX–Miscellaneous" or retyping the articles if there is not enough room. Typically, the additional clauses would be worded like this:

No person may be admitted to membership who is not
licensed to practice _____ in this state.
No interest in this company may be sold to anyone who
is not so licensed. Any member whose license to practice is revoked or terminated shall immediately
terminate his membership.

ADDITIONAL FORMS

Some states require forms to be filed in addition to the articles of organization. The following states require the forms listed. These requirements may change, so check with your state for additional requirements.

Arkansas	Franchise Tax Registration Form
California	Tax Voucher (form 3522)
D.C.	Consent of Registered Agent
Florida	Certificate of Designation of Registered Agent*
Georgia	Transmittal Form
Louisiana	Initial Report
Maine	Acceptance of Appointment as Registered Agent*
Michigan	If Form C&S 700 is not used for your articles it must accompany your articles.
New Hampshire	Addendum to Certificate of Formation
North Dakota	Registered Agent Consent to Serve
Ohio	Original Appointment of Agent
Pennsylvania	Docketing Statement DSCB: 15-134A
South Dakota	First Annual Report
Wyoming	Consent to Appointment of Registered Agent

*The information on these forms can be incorporated into the articles,
in which case the separate form does not need to be filed.

EXECUTION AND FILING

Some states allow any person to sign an LLC's articles of organization (even an agent or attorney), but others require a member or all the members to sign. Check the page for your state in Appendix A. To avoid delay in case your state's rules have changed, you can have all members sign even if it does not appear that it is required.

Some states require the form to be signed in black ink, but it is advisable for everyone to do so in case your state recently adopted the requirement. Most also require typing or printing.

Some states return the form quickly, while others normally take several weeks but will file it quicker for an additional charge. Some provide a street address for courier service (FedEx, Airborn) and will return by courier if you prepay.

PUBLICATION

A few states require a new LLC to publish notice of formation in a newspaper. Usually this must be in a "newspaper of general circulation." In most cases, a small inexpensive newspaper, or "shopper," can be used which will save hundreds of dollars over the rates of a big city daily newspaper. Check the page for your state in Appendix A for the requirements.

MEMBERSHIP OR MANAGEMENT AGREEMENT

As mentioned in the previous chapter, an LLC must decide if it will be managed by all the members or a limited number of managers. If it is to be run by managers, there may be one or more and he or she may be a member or not a member.

In either case, it is important to have a written agreement spelling out the rights and duties of the members and managers, if any. This is also a good document in which to include other rules governing the LLC. Even if an LLC has only one member, a membership agreement should be signed to formalize the LLC and make it clear that the member is not personally liable for the debts of the business.

The law of LLCs is very new and since corporations that do not follow procedures can have their "veil-pierced" (and their shareholders held liable), it is possible that a court may try the same on an LLC. So following the old formula is the safest. Of course, if you set up procedures and do not follow them, this could backfire and a court could use that as a reason to impose liability.

MEMBERSHIP OPERATING AGREEMENT
Form 6 in Appendix C is a generic **MEMBERSHIP OPERATING AGREEMENT**. Use this form if your LLC will have one member or if it will have two or more members and be managed by all the members.

This form has basic terms that can be useful to most businesses. If all of the terms apply to your business, you should execute a copy and keep it with your company records.

If there are other terms you would like to include in your agreement, you can add them in paragraph 21 or draw up an *addendum* to the membership agreement.

MANAGEMENT OPERATING AGREEMENT
Form 7 in Appendix C is a generic **MANAGEMENT OPERATIONS AGREEMENT**. Use this form if your LLC will have two or more members and be managed by a limited number of members or by someone who is not a member.

This form has basic terms which can be useful to most businesses. If all of the terms apply to your business, you should execute a copy and keep it with your company records.

If there are other terms you would like to include in your agreement, you can add them in paragraph 21 or draw up an addendum to the management agreement.

SCHEDULE A
The operating agreements both use a "Schedule A" to include the specific information for your company. (see form 8, p.163.)

CAPITALIZATION

Your new company will naturally need some money to get operations started. Some of this will be *capital* that you put into the business, but some may also be loans. Money that is set up as a loan can be later taken out tax-free. Therefore, it might seem good to start with all loans and little or no capital. But the danger is, if a business is *undercapitalized*, the owners may later be liable for some of its debts.

What is enough capital for a business is a legal question and no one can say what a judge or jury may some day decide. If the business is a service company and needs little equipment other than ladders or computers, a couple thousand dollars would be fine. If it is a business that needs a lot of expensive equipment, it would probably not be reasonable to put in $1,000 in capital and $99,000 in loans.

One way to know what is reasonable is to see what a bank would loan the company. If a company could put $5,000 down on its start-up equipment and borrow the rest, it would probably be reasonable to use $5,000 as capital and $95,000 as a loan from the owner.

If you are unsure if your intended capitalization is right, you could check a book on business accounting or with an accountant who works with start-up businesses.

If an existing business is being converted to an LLC, you may want to contribute the existing equipment as part, or all, of the start-up capital. To avoid potential liability, you should be sure not to value the equipment at more than the fair market value. To transfer the equipment to the company, you can use the BILL OF SALE in this book. (see form 5, p.157.)

In some instances, people wish to trade services for an interest in a business. For example, one person may contribute business equipment and the other work for three months without pay, for fifty-fifty ownership in the business. But in some states, this is not allowed. Check you state statute before setting up such an arrangement.

TAX FORMS

In forming an LLC, there are two tax forms you will need to complete; **IRS FORM SS-4** and **IRS FORM 8832**.

<small>TAXPAYER
IDENTIFICATION
NUMBER</small>

Prior to opening a bank account, the limited liability company must obtain a *taxpayer identification number*, which is the business equivalent of a social security number. This is done by filing **IRS FORM SS-4**. (see form 3, p.145.) If you mail it in, it may take two or three weeks. If you fax it in they will usually fax back your number in a few days. If you need the number more quickly you can obtain it by phone in about twenty to forty minutes, depening on how long you are on hold. Be sure to have your completed **IRS FORM SS-4** in front of you when you call. The address, phone and fax numbers are in the instructions with the form.

When you apply for this number, you will probably be put on the mailing list for other tax forms. If you do not receive these, you should call your local IRS forms number and request the forms for new businesses. These include Circular E explaining the taxes due, the W-4 forms for each employee, the tax deposit coupons and the Form 941 quarterly return for withholding.

<small>FORM 8832</small>

IRS FORM 8832 was issued by the IRS in 1997 to allow LLCs to chose their tax status. (see form 4, p.152.) It is basically a choice between partnership taxation and corporate taxation. For a single-member LLC, it is a choice between sole proprietorship taxation and corporate taxation.

The difference in taxation is that a sole proprietorship or partnership is not taxed at all, but a corporation is treated like a separate taxpayer. A sole proprietorship or partnership just reports its income and expenses and the proprietor or partners report the net profit or loss on their personal tax return. A corporation files a tax return and pays tax on any profits, and if it distributes any of the profits to the members, those profits are taxed again. Therefore, in most cases it is better not to choose corporate taxation.

One way around the double taxation is if all of the profits can be paid to the members as salary, they are deductible and the corporation has no profit on which to pay tax. The problem arises when the company makes more money than would be reasonable to pay as salaries. The IRS can then impose extra corporate taxation on the excess amounts.

If you are unsure how you wish to be taxed, you should consult a book on taxation of businesses or check with a tax professional. Once you decide, you should complete **IRS FORM 8832**. If you elect to pass through taxation, you do not need to file the form, just give it to the members to file with their annual returns. If you elect corporate taxation, you need to file the form within seventy-five days.

EMPLOYEES

An LLC that has employees other than its members is subject to numerous laws and reporting requirements which are beyond the scope of this book. These include new hire reporting, federal wage withholding, state and federal unemployment compensation taxes, discrimination laws, minimum wage laws, and numerous posters that must be placed in the workplace such as child labor laws and health and safety issues.

BANK ACCOUNTS

A limited liability company must have a bank account. Checks payable to a limited liability company cannot be cashed–they must be deposited into an account.

Unfortunately, many banks charge companies for the "right" to put their money in the bank. You can tell how much extra a company is being charged when you compare a corporate account to a personal account with similar activity. For similar balance and activity, an individual might earn $6.00 interest for the month while a corporation pays $40.00 in bank fees. The bank is not losing money on every personal account, so the corporate account is simply generating $46.00 more in profit for the bank.

Usually, there is a complicated scheme of fees with charges for each transaction. Many banks charge companies for the right to make a deposit. (Twenty-five cents for the deposit plus 10¢ for each check that is deposited. Deposit thirty checks and this will cost you $3.25.) The customer is often granted an interest credit on the balance in the account, but it is usually small and if the credit is larger than the charges, you lose the excess.

Fortunately, some banks have set up reasonable fees for small businesses such as charging no fees if a balance of $1000 or $2500 is maintained. Because the fees can easily amount to hundreds of dollars a year, it pays to shop around. Even if the bank is relatively far from the business, using bank-by-mail can make the distance meaningless. But don't be surprised if a bank with low fees raises them. The author knows of one company that changed banks four times in one year as each one raised its fees or was bought out by a bank with higher fees.

One method for avoiding high bank fees is to open a checking account and a *money market account*. (Money market accounts pay higher interest and usually do not charge for making deposits. You can only write three checks a month but you can usually make unlimited withdrawals.) Put all of your deposits into the money market account and just pay bills out of the regular checking account, transferring funds as needed. Some banks also charge for deposits into money market accounts, so start one at a brokerage firm.

Another way to save money in bank charges is to order checks from a private source rather than through the bank. These are usually much cheaper than those the bank offers because the bank makes a profit on the check printing. If the bank officer doesn't like the idea when you are opening the account, just wait until your first batch runs out and switch over without telling the bank. They probably won't even notice, as long as you get the checks printed correctly. Most "business checks" are large and expensive. There is no reason you cannot use small "personal size" checks for your business.

All you should need to open a company bank account is a copy of your articles of incorporation and your federal tax identification number. If you have trouble opening the account, you can use the BANKING RESOLUTION (see form 11, p.169) included with this book, or you can make up a similar form.

LICENSES

Counties and municipalities in most states are authorized to levy a license tax on the right to do business. Before opening your business, you should obtain a county occupational license, and if you will be working within a city, a city occupational license. Businesses that perform work in several cities, such as builders, must obtain a license from each city in which they work. This does not have to be done until you actually begin a job in a particular city.

County occupational licenses can usually be obtained from the tax collector in the county courthouse. City licenses are usually available at city hall. Be sure to find out if zoning allows your type of business before buying or leasing property because the licensing departments will check the zoning before issuing your license.

Problems occasionally arise when persons attempt to start a business in their home. Small new businesses cannot afford to pay rent for commercial space and cities often try to forbid business in residential areas. Getting a county occupational license often gives notice to the city that a business is being conducted in a residential area.

Some people avoid the problem by starting their businesses without occupational licenses, figuring that the penalties are nowhere near the cost of office space. Others get the county license and ignore the city rules. If a person has commercial trucks and equipment parked on his property, there will probably be complaints by neighbors and the city will most likely take legal action. But if a person's business consists merely of making phone calls out of the home and keeping supplies inside the house, the problem may never arise.

If a problem does occur regarding a home business that does not disturb the neighbors, a good argument can be made that the zoning law that prohibits the business is unconstitutional. When zoning laws were first instituted, they were not meant to stop people from doing things in a residence that had historically been part of the life in a residence. Consider a painter. Should a zoning law prohibit a person from sitting in his home and painting pictures? If he sells them for a living is there a difference? Can the government force him to rent commercial space?

Similar arguments can be made for many home businesses. But court battles with a city are expensive and probably not worth the effort for a small business. The best course of action is to keep a low profile. Using a post office box is sometimes helpful in diverting attention away from the residence. However, the secretary of state and the occupational license administrator will usually demand a street address. In most areas, there should be no problem using a residential address and explaining to the city that it is merely the corporate address and that no business is conducted on the premises. But in some areas, this is forbidden and strictly enforced.

CHECKLIST FOR FORMING AN LLC

❒ Decide on a company name

❒ Search the name to be sure it is not already taken

❒ Prepare and file ARTICLES OF ORGANIZATION and any other organizational form required by the state

❒ Decide on capitalization and tax status

❒ Obtain Federal Employer Identification Number (IRS FORM SS-4)

❒ Prepare IRS FORM 8832 and file it within seventy-five days *if* you are choosing corporate taxation.

❒ Prepare MEMBERSHIP OPERATING AGREEMENT or MANAGEMENT OPERATING AGREEMENT

❒ If necessary, meet with securities lawyer regarding nonparticipating members

❒ Hold organizational meeting

　　❒ Complete OPERATING AGREEMENT

　　❒ Complete BILL OF SALE if property is traded for interest

❒ File fictitious or assumed name registration if one will be used

❒ Get city or county licenses, if needed

❒ Open bank account

SELLING INTERESTS IN THE COMPANY 5

If you will have members of your LLC who will not participate in the business, you need to know about securities laws. If everyone will participate, you can skip this chapter.

SECURITIES LAWS

The issuance of securities is subject to both federal and state securities laws. A *security* can either be an equity interest in a company (stock, membership) or debt (notes, bonds, etc.). The laws covering securities are so broad that any instrument that represents an investment in an enterprise where the investor is relying on the efforts of others for profit is considered a security. Even a *promissory note* has been held to be a security. Once an investment is determined to involve a security, strict rules apply. There can be criminal penalties and civil damages can also be awarded to purchasers if the rules are not followed.

The rules are designed to protect people who put up money as an investment in a business. In the stock market crash in the 1930s many people lost their life savings in swindles, and the government wants to be sure that it won't happen again. Unfortunately, the laws can also make it difficult to raise capital for many honest businesses.

The goal of the laws covering sales of securities is that investors be given full disclosure of the risks involved in an investment. To accomplish this, the law usually requires that the securities must either be registered with the *Federal Securities and Exchange Commission* or a similar state regulatory body and that lengthy disclosure statements be compiled and distributed.

The law is complicated and strict compliance is required. The penalties are so harsh that most lawyers won't handle securities matters. You most likely would not be able to get through the registration process on your own. But, like your decision to form your LLC without a lawyer, you may wish to consider some alternatives when attempting to raise capital without a lawyer.

- Borrow the money as a personal loan from friends or relatives. The disadvantage is that you will have to pay them back personally if the business fails. However, you may have to do that anyway if they are close relatives or if you do not follow the securities laws.

- Tailor your stock issuance to fall within the exemptions in the securities laws. There are some exemptions in the securities laws for small businesses that may apply to your transaction. (The anti-fraud provisions always apply even if the transaction is exempt from registration.) Some exemptions are explained below, but you should make at least one appointment with a securities lawyer to be sure you have covered everything and that there have not been any changes in the law. Often, you can pay for an hour or so of a securities lawyer's time for $100 or $200 and just ask questions about your plans. He or she can tell you what not to do and what your options are. You can then make an informed decision.

FEDERAL EXEMPTIONS FROM SECURITIES LAWS

In most situations where one person, a husband and wife or a few partners run a business, and all parties are active in the enterprise, securities laws do not apply to their issuance of stock to themselves. As a practical matter, if your father or aunt wants to put up some money for some stock in your business, you might not get in trouble. They probably won't seek triple damages and criminal penalties if your business fails.

However, you may wish to obtain money from additional investors to enable your business to grow. This can be done in many circumstances as long as you follow the rules carefully. In some cases, you do not have to file anything with the Securities and Exchange Commission (SEC) but in others, you must file a notice.

FEDERAL PRIVATE PLACEMENT EXEMPTION

If you sell interests in your business to a small group of people without any advertising, you can fall into the private offering exemption if the following are true:

- all persons to whom offers are made are financially astute, are participants in the business, or have a substantial net worth;

- no advertising or general solicitation is used to promote the stock;

- the number of persons to whom the offers are made is limited;

- the shares are purchased for investment and not for immediate resale;

- the persons to whom the stock is offered are given all relevant information (including financial information) regarding the issuance and the corporation. Again, there are numerous court cases explaining each aspect of these rules, including such questions as what is a "financially astute" person; and,

- a filing claiming the exemption is made upon the United States Securities and Exchange Commission.

FEDERAL
INTRASTATE
OFFERING
EXEMPTION

If you only offer your securities to residents of one state you may be exempt from federal securities laws. This is because federal laws usually only apply to interstate commerce. Intrastate offerings are covered by SEC Rule 147 and, if it is followed carefully, your sale will be exempt from federal registration.

FEDERAL SMALL
OFFERINGS
EXEMPTIONS

In recent years the SEC has liberalized the rules in order to make it easier for business to grow. Under Regulation D adopted by the Securities and Exchange Commission, there are three types of exemptions under rules 504, 505 and 506.

- The offering of securities of up to $1,000,000 in a twelve month period can be exempt under SEC Rule 504. Offers can be made to any number of persons, no specific information must be provided and investors do not have to be sophisticated.

- Under SEC Rule 505 offering of up to $5,000,000 can be made in a twelve month period but no public advertising may be used and only thirty-five non-accredited investors may purchase stock. Any number of *accredited investors* may purchase stock. (Accredited investors are sophisticated individuals with high net worth or high income, large trusts or investment companies, or persons involved in the business.)

- SEC Rule 506 has no limit on the amount of money that may be raised but, like Rule 505, does not allow advertising and limits non-accredited investors to thirty-five.

STATE SECURITIES LAWS

One reason there are exemptions from federal securities laws is that there are so many state laws covering securities that additional registration is not needed. Every state has securities laws, which are called *blue sky laws*. If you wish to offer your stock in all fifty states, you must be registered in all fifty states unless you can fit into one of the exemptions. However, exemptions are very limited.

TYPICAL STATE
LAW PRIVATE
PLACEMENT
EXEMPTION

The most common one is the private placement exemption. This can apply if all of the following are true:

- there are thirty-five or fewer purchasers of shares;

- no commissions are paid to anyone to promote the stock;

- no advertising or general solicitation is used to promote the stock;

- all material information (including financial information) regarding the stock issuance and the company is given or is accessible to all shareholders; and,

- a three day right of recision is given.

These rules may sound simple on the surface, but there are many more rules, regulations, and court cases explaining each one in more detail. For example, what does "thirty-five persons" mean? Sounds simple, but it can mean more than thirty-five persons. Spouses, persons whose *net worth* exceeds a million dollars, and founders of the company may not be counted in some circumstances.

As you can see, the exemption doesn't give you much latitude in raising money. Therefore, if you wish to raise money from a wider group of people, you will have to register. To find out more about your state's requirements, you should contact the securities commission of your state. The address is in the back of this chapter.

BLUE SKY
REPORTER

Another good source of information concerning the securities laws of all fifty states is the *Blue Sky Reporter*, a multi-volume loose leaf service which summarizes the securities laws of the states. A copy should be available in most law libraries.

INTERNET STOCK SALES

With the advent of the Internet, promoters of business interests have a new way of reaching large numbers of people. However, all securities laws apply to the Internet and they are being enforced. Recently, state attorneys general have issued cease and desist orders to promoters not registered in their states.

Under current law, you must be registered in a state in order to sell stock to its residents. You must turn down any residents from a state who want to buy your stock if you are not registered in that state.

You may wonder how the famous Spring Street Brewing raised $1.6 million for its Wit Beer on the Internet. The main reason they were successful was because their president is a securities lawyer and could prepare his own prospectus to file with the SEC and the states. That would have cost anyone else about $100,000. Also, most of their stock sales were inspired by newspaper and magazine articles about them and not from the Internet.

The lawyer who marketed Wit Beer's shares on the Internet has started a business to advise others on raising capital. It is Wit Capital located at 826 Broadway, 6th Floor, New York, NY 10003.

Some Internet sites that may be helpful in raising capital are:

America's Business Funding Directory: www.businessfinance.com
Angel Capital Electronic Network (SBA): www.sba.gov
FinanceHub: www.financehub.com
NVST: www.nvst.com

PAYMENT FOR MEMBERSHIP INTERESTS

When issuing stock, it is important that full payment be made by the purchasers. If the shares have a par value and the payment is in cash, the cash must not be less than the par value. In most states, promissory notes cannot be used in payment for shares. The shares must not be issued until the payment has been received by the corporation.

TRADING PROPERTY FOR INTERESTS

In many cases, organizers of a corporation have property they want to contribute for use in starting up the business. This is often the case where an on-going business is incorporated. To avoid future problems, the property should be traded at a fair value for the shares. The directors should pass a resolution stating that they agree with the value of the property. When the stock certificate is issued in exchange for the property, a bill of sale should be executed by the owner of the property detailing everything which is being exchanged for the stock.

TAXABLE
TRANSACTIONS

In cases where property is exchanged for something of value, such as stock, there is often income tax due as if there had been a sale of the property. Fortunately, Section 351 of the IRS Code allows tax-free exchange of property for stock if the persons receiving the stock for the property or for cash *end up owning* at least eighty percent of the voting and other stock in the corporation. If more than twenty percent of the stock is issued in exchange for services instead of property or cash, the transfers of property will be taxable and treated as a sale for cash.

TRADING
SERVICES FOR
INTERESTS

In some cases, the founders of an LLC wish to issue membership interests to one or more persons in exchange for their services to the business. It has always been possible to issue interests for services which have previously been performed. Some states make it unlawful to issue interests for promises to perform services in the future. Check your state's LLC statutes if you plan to do this.

State Securities Registration Offices

The following are the addresses of the state offices that handle registration of securities. You can contact them for information on their requirements.

Alabama Securities Commission
770 Washington Street, Suite 570
Montgomery, AL 36130-4700
Phone: 334-242-2984 or 800-222-1253
Fax: 334-242-0240 or 334-353-4690

**Alaska Department of Commerce
and Economic Development
Division of Banking, Securities,
and Corporations**
P.O. Box 110807
Juneau, AK 99811-0807
Phone: 907-465-2521
Fax: 907-465-2549
www.dced.state.ak.us/bsc

**Arizona Corporation Commission
Securities Division**
1300 West Washington Street, 3d Floor
Phoenix, AZ 85007
Phone: 602-542-4242
Fax: 602-542-3583
www.ccsd.cc.state.az.us

Arkansas Securities Department
Heritage West Building
201 East Markham, Suite 300
Little Rock, AR 72201
Phone: 501-324-9260
Fax: 501-324-9268

**California Department of Corporations
Securities Regulation Division**
320 West 4th Street, Suite 750
Los Angeles, California 90013-2344
Phone: 213-736-3482
Fax: 213-736-3588
www.corp.ca.gov/srd/security.htm

Colorado Division of Securities
1580 Lincoln Street, Suite 420
Denver, CO 80203
Phone: 303-894-2320
Fax: 303-861-2126
www.dora.state.co.us/securities

Connecticut Securities Division
260 Constitution Plaza
Hartford, CT 06106-1800
Phone: 806-240-8230
Fax: 860-240-8178
www.state.ct.us/dob/

**Delaware Department of Justice
Division of Securities**
820 N. French Street, 5th Floor
Wilmington, DE 19801
Phone: 302-577-2515
Fax: 302-655-0576
www.state.de.us/securities/index.htm

**District of Columbia
Department of Insurance and
Securities Regulation**
810 First Street, Suite 701
Washington, DC 20002
Phone: 202-727-8000
Fax: 202-783-3571
www.disr.washingtondc.gov/main.shtm

Florida Division of Securities and Finance
101 E. Gaines Street
Tallahassee, FL 32399-0350
Phone: 850-488-9805
Fax: 850-681-2428
www.dbf.state.fl.us/licensing

Georgia Secretary of State
Securities and Business
Regulation Division
2 Martin Luther King Jr. Drive
Suite 802, West Tower
Atlanta, GA 30334
Phone: 404-656-3920
Fax: 404-657-8410
www.SOS.State.Ga.US/Securities/
or www.georgiasecurities.org

Hawaii Department of Commerce
and Consumer Affairs
Commissioner of Securities
P. O. Box 40
Honolulu, HI 96810
Phone: 808-586-2744
Fax: 808-586-2733
www.state.hi.us/dcca/breq-seu/
compliance.html

Idaho Department of Finance
700 W. State Street, 2nd Floor,
P.O. Box 83720
Boise, ID 83720-0031
Phone: 208-334-2441
Fax: 208-332-8099
www.state.id.us./finance/dof.htm

Illinois Securities Department
Lincoln Tower, Suite 200
520 South Second Street
Springfield, Illinois 62701
Phone: 217-782-2256
Fax: 217-782-8876
www.sos.state.il.us/departments/
securities/securities.html

Indiana Securities Division
302 West Washington Street, Room E-111
Indianapolis, IN 46204
Phone: 317-232-6687 or 800-223-8791
Fax: 317-233-3675
www.IN.gov/sos/securities

Iowa Securities Bureau
Lucas State Office Building, Room 214
Agency Des Moines, IA 50319
Phone: 515-281-4441
Fax: 515-281-6467
www.state.ia.us/

Kansas Securities Commissioner
Office of the Securities Commissioner
618 South Kansas Avenue
Topeka, KS 66603
Phone: 785-296-3307
Fax: 785-296-6872
www.ink.org/public/ksccom

Kentucky Department of
Financial Institutions
1025 Capital Center Drive, Suite 200
Frankfort, KY 40601-3868
Phone: 502-573-3390 or 800-223-2579
Fax: 502-573-8787
www.dfi.state.ky.us

Louisiana Office of Financial Institutions
Securities Division
P.O. Box 94095
Baton Rouge, LA 70804-9095
Phone: 225-925-4660
Fax: 225-925-4548
www.ofi.state.la.us/

Maine Securities Division
Office of Securities
121 State House Station
Bureau of Banking
Augusta, ME 04333
Phone: 207-624-8551
Fax: 207-624-8590
www.state.me.us/pfr/sec/sec_index.htm

Maryland Securities Division
200 Saint Paul Place 20th Floor
Baltimore, MD 21202
Phone: 410-576-6360
www.oaq.state.md.us/securities
/index.htm

Massachusetts Securities Division
One Ashburton Place, 17th Floor
Boston, MA 02108
Phone: 617-727-3548 or 800-269-5428
Fax: 617-248-0177
www.state.ma.us/sec/sct/sctidx.htm

**Michigan Department of
Consumer and Industry Services
Offices of Financial and
Insurance Services**
P.O. Box 30222
Lansing, MI 48909-7720
Phone: 517-373-0220 or 877-999-6442
Fax: 517-335-4978
www.cis.state.mi.us/ofis

Minnesota Department of Commerce
85 7th Place East, Suite 500
St. Paul, MN 55101
Phone: 651-296-4973
www.commerce.state.mn.us/pages/
securitiesmain.htm

Mississippi Securities Division
P.O. Box 136
Jackson, MS 39205
Phone: 601-359-1350
Fax: 601-359-1499
www.sos.state.ms.us/busserv/
securities/securities.html

**Office of the Missouri Secretary of State
Securities Division**
600 West Main St., 2nd Floor
Jefferson City, MO 65101
www.sos.state.mo.ps/securities
/default.asp

**Montana Office of the State Auditor
Securities Division**
P.O. Box 4009
Helena, MT 59604-4009
Phone: 406-444-5222
Fax: 406-444-5558
www.state.mt.us/sao/securities/
properly_liscensed.htm

Nebraska Bureau of Securities
The Atrium, Suite 311
1200 N Street
P.O. Box 95006
Lincoln, NE 68509-5006
Phone: 402-471-3445
www.ndbf.org/sec.htm

Nevada Securities Division
555 E. Washington Avenue, Suite 5200
Las Vegas, NV 89101
Phone: 702-486-2440
Fax: 702-486-2452
www.sos.state.nv.us/securities/index.htm

**New Hampshire Bureau of
Securities Regulation**
State House, Room 204
Concord, NH 03301-4989
Phone: 603-271-1463
Fax: 603-271-7933
webster.state.nh.us/sos/securities

New Jersey Bureau of Securities
153 Halsey Street
P.O. Box 47029
Newark, NJ 07101
Phone: 973-504-3600
www.state.nj.us/lps/ca/bocs.htm

**New Mexico Securities Division
Regulation and Licensing Department**
725 St. Michaels Drive
Santa Fe, NM 87505
Phone: 505-827-7140
www.rld.state.nm.us/sec/index.htm

**New York State
Attorney General's Office**
120 Broadway, 23rd. Floor
New York, NY 10271
Phone: 212-416-8200
Fax: 212-416-8222
www.oag.state.ny.us/investors
/investors.html

**North Carolina Securities Division
Department of the Secretary of State**
P.O. Box 29622
Raleigh, NC 27626-0622
Phone: 919-733-3924
Fax: 919-733-5172
www.secretary.state.nc.us/sec

North Dakota Securities Commission
State Capitol, 5th Floor
600 East Avenue
Bismarck, ND 58505-0510
Phone: 701-328-2910
Fax: 701-328-2946
www.state.nd.us/securities/

**Ohio Department of Commerce
Division of Securities**
77 South High Street, 22nd. Floor
Columbus, OH 43215
Phone: 614-644-7381
www.securities.state.oh.us/

**Oklahoma Department of Securities
First National Center**
120 North Robinson, Suite 860
Oklahoma City, OK 73102
Phone: 405-280-7700
Fax: 405-280-7742
www.securities.state.ok.us

**Oregon Department of Consumer
and Business Services
Division of Finance and
Corporate Securities**
350 Winter Street NE, Room 410
Salem, OR 97301-3880
Phone: 503-378-4140
Fax: 503-947-7862
www.cbs.state.or.us/external/dfcs

**Pennsylvania Division of
Corporation Finance
Pennsylvania Securities Commission**
Eastgate Office Building, 2nd Floor,
1010 North 7th Street
Harrisburg, PA 17102-1410
Phone: 717-787-8061
Fax: 717-783-5122
www.psc.state.pa.us/

**Puerto Rico Commissioner of
Financial Institutions**
Centro Europa Building
1492 Ponce de Leon Avenue, Suite 600
San Juan, PR 00907-4127
Phone: 787-723-8445
Fax: 787-723-3857
www.cif.gov.pr/html/securities.html

South Carolina Securities Division
P.O. Box 11350
Columbia, SC 29211
Phone: 803-734-9916
www.scsecurities.org/index.html

South Dakota Division of Securities
118 West Capital
Pierre, SD 57501
Phone: 605-773-4823
Fax: 605-773-5953
www.state.sd.us/dcr/securities
/security.htm

Tennessee Department of Commerce and Insurance Securities Division
500 James Robertson Parkway, Suite 680
Nashville, TN 37243-0583
Phone: 615-741-3187
Fax: 615-532-8375
www.state.tn.us/commerce
/securdiv.html

Texas State Securities Board
P.O. Box 13167
Austin, Texas 78711-3167
Phone: 512-305-8300
Fax: 512-305-8310
www.ssb.state.tx.us

Utah Department of Commerce Division of Securities
Box 146760
Salt Lake City, Utah 84114-6766
Phone: 801-530-6600
Fax: 801-530-6980
www.securities.state.ut.us

Vermont Securities Division Department of Banking, Insurance, Securities and Health Care Administration
89 Main Street
Drawer 20
Montpelier, VT 05620-3101
Phone: 802-828-3420
www.bishca.state.vt.us/securitiesdiv
/securindex.htm

Virginia State Corporation Commission
P.O. Box 1197
Richmond, VA 23218
Phone: 804-371-9051
Fax: 804-371-9911
www.states.va.us/scc/division/srf/
webpages/homepagejavab.htm

Washington Department of Financial Institutions Securities Division
P.O. Box 9033
Olympia, Washington 98507-9033
Phone: 360-902-8766
Fax: 360-586-5068
www.dfi.wa.gov/sd/default.htm

West Virginia Securities Division
State Capitol Building 1
Room W-100
Charleston, WV 25305
Phone: 304-558-2257
Fax: 304-558-4211
www.wvauditor.com

Wisconsin Division of Securities
P.O. Box 1768
Madison, WI 53701-1768
Phone: 608-266-1064
Fax: 608-264-7979
www.wdfi.org/fi/securities

Wyoming Securities Division Secretary of the State
State Capital Building
Cheyenne, WY 82002-0020
Phone: 307-777-7378
Fax: 307-777-6217
http://soswy.state.wy.us/securiti
/securiti.htm

RUNNING A LIMITED LIABILITY COMPANY 6

One benefit of the limited liability company is the lack of requirements needed to comply with the formalities of a corporation. However, since the entity is so new it is not yet clear what, if any, requirements courts may impose. Though it is widely recognized that the requirements will be less strict than for a corporation, to be safe it is best to have some formalities such as keeping minutes and records.

DAY-TO-DAY ACTIVITIES

As previously mentioned, every LLC should have an operating agreement. This usually contains some formalities for the operation of the company. The important thing is that, if there are formalities in the document, you should follow them.

MINUTES In most states the keeping of minutes is not specifically required of an LLC, but it is a simple act which may be helpful in proving that the LLC followed enough formalities to be legitimate. Whenever the company takes some major action, such as leasing a new office or granting bonuses, you should prepare minutes reflecting the decision. A blank MINUTES form is included in this book that does not take much time to fill out. (see form 9, p.165.) Keep several blank copies with your company papers—this way, you will have them on hand when you need them.

One important point to remember is to keep the company separate from your personal affairs. Do not continuously make loans to yourself from company funds and do not commingle funds.

Another important point to remember is to always use the name of the company with the correct suffix (LLC, LC, etc.). Always sign company documents as a member of the company acting for the company, like this:

Happy Daze L.L.C.

By___*Joe Daze*_____Member

If you do not, you may lose your protection from liability. There have been cases where a person forgot to put his title after his name and was held personally liable for a company debt!

Member Meetings

There is no requirement for regular meetings of the members. But, once again, since the law is not settled in this area, the more formality you use, the greater protection you have.

Holding a meeting when major decisions are being made is a good idea. If you are a one-member company you can hold the meeting in your head. Just remember to fill out a minutes form and put it with the company records.

Records

Each state has its own statute controlling whether or not records need to be kept and if so, what types. A summary for each state is included in Appendix A. However, since the laws may change you should get a copy of the section of your state's law to be sure you are in compliance. Typically the following types of things need to be kept on file:

- a current list of the names and last known addresses of all - members;

- a copy of the articles of organization, plus any amendments;

- copies of the company's income tax returns for the last three years;

- copies of any regulations or member agreements currently in effect;

- copies of any financial statements for the company for the last three years; and,

- the amount of cash and the agreed value of any property or services contributed by each member or agreed to be contributed by each member.

ANNUAL REPORTS

In most states, an LLC must file a report each year (or in some states every two years). This is to let the state keep an up-to-date record of the status of the company and in many states the fee is small. But in some states, the annual report is a way to raise revenue and the fee is hundreds of dollars.

In most states, the report is a preprinted form with the company name, address, and member names which needs to be signed and returned.

Failure to file your annual report on time can result in your company being dissolved. In some states the fee for reinstatement is over $500, so do not miss the deadline!

AMENDING A LIMITED LIABILITY COMPANY

7

It is usually advisable to draft your LLC documents in broad enough language so that they cover most situations which may arise. However, when there are major changes in the LLC, you may have to amend some of your documents.

ARTICLES OF ORGANIZATION

Since the ARTICLES OF ORGANIZATION are on file with the secretary of state or other filing office, any amendments to them will have to also be filed and a filing fee paid. In some states, the fee is quite high, so if you can accomplish your changes without amending the articles it would save time and money.

REQUIRED
AMENDMENTS

To prepare an amendment, you should first check your state's statute to be sure that you include all information required and to see if it must be notarized or comply with any other requirements.

There are certain types of changes, such as a change of the company name or registered agent, for which you are required to file an amendment. In general, these are any things contained in the original articles of organization.

RESTATED
ARTICLES

Some states allow you to file "restated articles." This is usually done when a company has had several amendments to its articles and wishes to write a fresh copy deleting obsolete clauses and incorporating new clauses.

RAISING CAPITAL CONTRIBUTIONS

In some states, you are required to amend the articles if you change the capital contributions. This may require a substantial filing fee. A cheaper alternative would be to make a loan to the company rather than increase capital. But check with your accountant, or review a good tax guide to be sure the company is not undercapitalized.

MEMBERSHIP OR MANAGEMENT AGREEMENT

Your membership agreement or management agreement should contain a section spelling out the procedure for making amendments. Be sure to follow this procedure when making amendments. Otherwise, a court could use your failure as a reason to impose liability on the members.

REGISTERED AGENT OR REGISTERED OFFICE

If your registered agent or registered office changes, you must file this information as soon as it is effective and pay a filing fee. Many states have a form on which to do this. In case you neglect to do so, in most states, you can include the change on your annual report. By waiting until your annual report is due to make the change you may be able to avoid an extra filing fee. (But in some states you have to pay extra to change the agent.)

MERGING WITH ANOTHER BUSINESS

Merging with another business is usually somewhat complicated from both a tax and legal standpoint. Many states have extensive merger requirements in their LLC statutes. Before executing your plan, be sure to learn the tax implications and to check the statutes for the requirements.

DISSOLVING A LIMITED LIABILITY COMPANY   8

At some point you may decide to dissolve your LLC. This chapter explains the ways it can be done.

AUTOMATIC DISSOLUTION

If your limited liability company has ceased to do business and you no longer need to keep it active, in most states it is not necessary to take any special action to dissolve it. It will be automatically dissolved if you fail to file your annual report. If you decide to let your company dissolve this way, be sure that you won't need the company again because the fees for reinstatement can be high. You may need to pay annual fees for all previous years plus a penalty. The penalty can amount to several hundred dollars.

If your company has some debts that it is unable to pay at the time of dissolution, you would be better off formally dissolving it or having it file bankruptcy. Otherwise, there is a chance you could be held personally liable for the debts.

EVENTS REQUIRING DISSOLUTION

In some states, there are specific events which require an LLC to dissolve. Two examples are if it has a set term which has expired, or if a member dies and there is no provision for continuation after death. In the few remaining states which still require two members, the withdrawal of one would also require dissolution. In cases like these, the remaining members are usually required to file a form which formally dissolves the company.

ARTICLES OF DISSOLUTION

An advantage of formal dissolution is that, in most cases, if you give proper notice to creditors, after a period of time there is no risk that they can come back against the members.

To formally dissolve a limited liability company, *articles of dissolution* are usually filed with the secretary of state. The procedure varies somewhat by state so check your state's statute for specific requirements.

After dissolution, an LLC may not carry on business, but in many states it can continue its existence for the purpose of:

- collecting its assets;

- disposing of property which will not be distributed to members;

- discharging liabilities;

- distributing assets to creditors and members; and,

- doing anything else necessary to winding up its affairs.

REVOCATION OF DISSOLUTION

In some states, an LLC may "undissolve" within a certain length of time after filing articles of dissolution by filing *articles of revocation of dissolution.* Check your state statute if you need to do this.

JUDICIAL DISSOLUTION

A court may dissolve an LLC under certain circumstances. This can usually be initiated by a legal department of the state, a creditor, a member, or the LCC itself. State law controls this type of action, but there is also a chance that one of the parties can bring the business into bankruptcy court which is controlled by federal bankruptcy laws.

DISTRIBUTION OF ASSETS

When an LLC dissolves, its assets must be distributed as required by state law. In most cases, this will include:

- creditors, including members who are creditors;
- members and creators in satisfaction of liabilities; and,
- members in proportion to their capital accounts.

See your state's statute for more information.

BANKRUPTCY

If your company is in debt beyond its means, it can file for bankruptcy. Chapter 7 bankruptcy is for liquidation in which all of the assets of the company are sold and divided among the preferred creditors. Chapter 11 is for reorganization of debts where the company hopes that by extending the payment terms of its obligations it can eventually pay them and continue its business.

If an LLC files bankruptcy, this does not have to affect the credit of the members unless they have guaranteed some of the debts. In this case, they would have to either take over the debts or file bankruptcy themselves.

If the debts are small and there is little chance the creditors will pursue collection, bankruptcy is unnecessary. In this case, you can allow the state to dissolve the corporation for failure to file the annual report. However, if the debts are large and you fear the creditors will attempt to collect the debt from the members, you should go through formal bankruptcy and dissolution. Such a scenario is beyond the scope of this book and you should consult an attorney or bankruptcy manual for further guidance.

FOR FURTHER
REFERENCE

The following books provide in-depth analysis of LLC law. Some are expensive, but may be found in larger law libraries.

Bromberg, Alan R. and Ribstein, Larry E. *Bromberg and Ribstein on Limited Liability Partnerships and the Revised Uniform Partnership Act*. Aspen Law and Business, 2000.

Callison, J. William, and Maureen A. Sullivan. *Limited Liability Companies: A State by State Guide to Law and Practice*. Eagan: West Group, 1999.

Cunningham, John M. *Drafting Limited Liability Company Operating Agreements*. New York: Aspen Publishers, 1998.

Rubenstein, Jeffrey C., et al. *Limited Liability Companies: Law, Practice, and Forms*. Seattle: Shepards, 1992.

GLOSSARY

The following definitions explain how the words are used in this book. They may have other meanings in other contexts.

A

accredited investor. Sophisticated individuals with high net worth or high income, large trusts or investment companies, or persons involved in the business.

addendum. A document attached to another document to add some new terms.

articles of organization. The legal document used to form a limited liability company that sets out basic information about it, such as its name.

assignment. The transfer of legal rights to another person or entity.

B

blue sky laws. Laws governing the sales of securities.

C

C corporation. A corporation that pays taxes on its profits.

capital. Initial funding of the business.

charging order. A court order directed at an interest in an LLC.

corporation. An artificial legal person that is set up to conduct a business owned by shareholders and run by officers and directors.

D

dissolution. The closing of a limited liability company.

distributions. Money paid out to owners of a corporation or limited liability company.

E

employee. Person who works for another under that person's control and direction.

employer identification number. Number issued by the Internal Revenue Service to identify taxpayers who do not have social security numbers.

F

fictitious name. A name used by a business that is not its personal or legal name.

G

general partnership. A business that is owned by two or more persons.

I

independent contractor. A person who does work as a separate business rather than as an employee.

industry code. A number assigned to each type of business.

insolvent. Being without enough assets of income to pay debts.

L

legal person. An entity recognized by the state as a person apart from its members.

liability. The legal responsibility to pay for an injury.

licensing board. A government entity which grants permission to perform certain functions.

limited liability. Fixing the amount a person can be forced to pay for a legal event at a limited sum.

limited liability company. An artificial legal person set up to conduct a business owned and run by members.

limited liability partnership. An artificial legal person set up to conduct a business owned and run by members, which is set up for professionals such as attorneys or doctors.

limited partnership. A business that is owned by two or more persons of which one or more is liable for the debts of the business and one or more has no liability for the debts.

M

management agreement. The document that controls the operation of a limited liability company that is managed by managers.

manager. A person who controls the operations of a limited liability company.

manager-managed LLC. A limited liability company that is controlled by one or more managers who are not all of the members of the company.

member. Person owning an interest in a limited liability company.

member-managed LLC. A limited liability company that is controlled by all of its members.

minority interest owners. The owners of an interest in an LLC who own less than a majority interest.

minutes. Records of the proceedings of business meetings.

N

natural person. A human being as opposed to a legal person created by the law.

net worth. The value of a person or an entity after subtracting liabilities from assets.

O

occupational license. A government-issued permit to transact business.

operating agreement. A contract among members of a limited liability company spelling out how the company is to be run.

organizational meeting. The meeting of the founders of a corporation or limited liability company in which company is structured and ready to begin business.

P

partnership. A business formed by two or more persons.

personal liability. Being forced to pay for a liability out of personal funds rather than from limited company assets.

piercing the corporate veil. When a court ignores the corporate structure to hold the owners of the business liable.

promissory note. A legal document in which a person promises to pay a sum of money.

promoters. Persons who start a business venture and usually offer interests for sale to investors.

proprietorship. A business that is owned by one person.

provisions. Terms of a legal document.

R

registered agent. A person who is designated by a limited liability company to receive legal papers for the company.

registered office. A physical location where the registered agent of a limited liability company can receive legal papers for the company.

regulations. The former name of the operating agreement of a limited liability company.

S

S corporation. A corporation in which the profits are taxed to the shareholders.

securities. Interests in a business such as stock or bonds.

T

tax basis. The amount used as the cost of an item for tax purposes.

trademark. A name or symbol used to identify the source of goods or services.

U

undercapitalized. Not having enough money to soundly operate.

unemployment compensation. Payments to a former employee who was terminated from a job for a reason not based on his or her fault.

uniform business report. A form filed annually by an LLC in some states.

Z

zoning. Laws that regulate the use of real estate.

Appendix A
State-by-State LLC Statutes

The following pages contain a listing of each state's limited liability company laws and fees. Because the laws are constantly being changed by state legislatures, you should call before filing your papers to confirm the fees and other requirements. The phone numbers are provided for each state.

With the continued growth of the Internet, more and more state corporation divisions are making their forms, fees, and requirements available online. Some states have downloadable forms available, and some even allow you to search their entire database from the comfort of your home or office.

The current websites at the time of publication of this book are included for each state. However, the sites change constantly, so you may need to look a little deeper if your state's site has changed its address.

ALABAMA

Secretary of State
Corporate Section
P.O. Box 5616
Montgomery, AL 36130-5616
334-242-5324

Website: www.sos.state.al.us

State sends material within three weeks.

WHAT THEY SUPPLY:

State provides fill-in-the-blank Articles of Organization with short instructions and a help sheet.

WHAT MUST BE FILED:

You must file the original and two copies of the Articles of Organization in the county where the LLC's registered office is located. The Probate Court Judge will receive and record the original Articles. Within thirty days of filing, a completed Report (provided by the secretary of state with the filing package) must be filed with the Judge of Probate ($5 filing fee).

NAME REQUIREMENTS:

The name must contain the words "Limited Liability Company" or "L.L.C."

A name reservation for an LLC is not possible.

ARTICLES SPECIAL REQUIREMENTS:

The Articles must set forth the rights, terms and conditions to admit additional members, and, if given, the right by remaining members to continue business after dissociation.

FILING FEES:

There is a filing fee of $40, payable to the "Secretary of State" plus an additional $35 filing fee for the Probate Court Judge (separate check).

REPORTS:

As stated above, the first report must be filed within thirty days after filing the Articles of Organization with a $5 fee with the Judge of Probate.

RECORDS REQUIRED:

- Names and addresses of members and managers
- Articles and all amendments
- Three years of financial records
- Three years of tax returns
- Operating agreement and all amendments

STATUTES:

Code of Alabama, Title 10, Chapter 12, Alabama Limited Liability Company Act.

ALASKA

Department of Commerce and Economic
Development
Division of B.S.C.
Attention: Corporation Section
P.O. Box 110808
Juneau, AK 99811-0807
907-465-2530
Fax: 907-465-2549

Website:
www.dced.state.ak.us

State sends material within three weeks.

WHAT THEY SUPPLY:

General information on forming a LLC under the
Alaska Limited Liability Act, as well as instructions
on filing the Articles of Organization. State provides
fill-in-the-blank Articles of Organization form and
the Standard Industrial Classification (S.I.C.) code to
determine the LLC's purpose.

WHAT MUST BE FILED:

An original and an exact copy of the fill-in-the-blank
Articles of Organization. The Articles should contain
a statement that they are being filed under the provisions of the Alaska Limited Liability Act.

NAME REQUIREMENTS:

The name must contain the words "limited liability
company" or the abbreviation "LLC." The name may
not contain the word "city" or "borough," or otherwise
imply that the company is a municipality. The name
must be distinguishable from trade names on record
with the Division of Banking, Securities and
Corporations.

ARTICLES SPECIAL REQUIREMENTS:

The purpose of the LLC must be characterized with
at least two S.I.C. code numbers which are listed in
the chart on the next page.

FILING FEES:

The filing fee is $250 which includes a biennial
license fee of $100. The fee is payable to the "State of
Alaska."

REPORTS:

An LLC Company Report must be filed every two
years with a $100 biennial fee. The report must be
delivered before January 2 each year.

RECORDS REQUIRED:

- Names and addresses of members and managers
- Articles and all amendments
- Three years of financial records
- Three years of tax returns
- Operating agreement and all amendments

STATUTES:

Alaska Statutes, Title 10, beginning with Section 50.010,
Alaska Limited Liability Act.

BUSINESS CLASSIFICATION CODES

AGRICULTURE, FORESTRY & FISHING

0100   Agricultural Production - Crops
0200   Agricultural Production - Livestock
0700   Agricultural Services (Inc. Animal, Livestock & Landscape Services)
0800   Forestry
0900   Fishing, Hunting & Trapping

MINING

1000   Metal Mining
1200   Coal Mining
1300   Oil & Gas Extraction
1400   Mining and Quarrying of Nonmetallic Minerals, except Fuels

CONSTRUCTION

1500   General Building Contractors
1600   Heavy Construction other than Building Construction Contractor
1700   Special Trade Construction Contractors
1800   Construction Exempt from Contractor Licensing

MANUFACTURING

2000   Food & Kindred Products
2100   Tobacco Manufacturers
2200   Textile Mill Products
2300   Apparel & Other Textile Products
2400   Lumber & Wood Products, except Furniture
2500   Furniture & Fixtures
2600   Paper & Allied Products
2700   Printing & Publishing and Allied Industries
2800   Chemicals & Allied Products
2900   Petroleum refining and related Industries
3000   Rubber & Misc. Plastic Products
3100   Leather & Leather Products
3200   Stone, Clay, Glass & COncrete Products
3300   Primary Metal Industries
3400   Fabricated Metal Products except Machinery and Transportation Equipment
3500   Industrial/Commercial Machinery & Computer Equipment
3600   Electronic & Other Electrical Equipment & Components except Computer Equipment
3700   Transportation Equipment
3800   Measuring, Analyzing & Controlling
3900   Misc. Manufacturing Industries

TRANSPORTATION & PUBLIC UTILITIES

4000   Railroad Transportation
4100   Local & Suburban Transit & Interurban
4200   Motor Freight Transportation & Warehousing
4300   U.S. Postal Service
4400   Water Transportation
4500   Air Transportation
4600   Pipelines, Except Natural Gas
4700   Transportation Services
4800   Communication
4900   Electric, Gas & Sanitary Services

WHOLESALE TRADE

5000   Wholesale Trade - Durable Goods
5100   Wholesale Trade - Nondurable Goods

RETAIL TRADE

5200   Building Materials, Hardware, Garden Supply & Mobile Home Dealers
5300   General Merchandise Stores
5400   Food Stores
5500   Automotive Dealers & Gasoline Service Stations
5600   Apparel & Accessory Stores
5700   Home Furniture, Furnishing & Equipment Stores
5800   Eating & Drinking Places
5900   Miscellaneous Retail

FINANCE, INSURANCE & REAL ESTATE

6000   Depository Institutions
6100   Nondepository Credit Institutions
6200   Security & Commodity Brokers, Dealers Exchanges & Services
6300   Insurance Carriers
6400   Insurance Agents, Brokers, and Service
6500   Real Estate
6700   Holding & Other Investment Offices

SERVICES

7000   Hotels, Rooming Houses, Camps & Other Lodging Places
7200   Personal services
7300   Business Services
7500   Auto Repair Services & Parking
7600   Misc. Repair Services
7800   Motion Pictures
7900   Amusement & Recreation Services
8000   Health Services
8100   Legal Services
8200   Educational Services
8300   Social Services
8400   Museums, Art Galleries & Botanical & Zoological Gardens
8600   Membership Organizations
8700   Engineering, Accounting, Research, Management & Related Services
8800   Private Households (Domestic Services)
8999   Misc. Services, not elsewhere classified (Artists, Writers)

ARIZONA

Arizona Corporation Commission
1300 W. Washington, 1st Floor
Phoenix, AZ 85007-2929
602-542-3135
800-345-5819 (Arizona residents only)
or
400 W. Congress
Tucson, AZ 85701-1347
520-628-6560

Website: www.cc.state.az.us

WHAT THEY SUPPLY:

State provides duplicate filing package containing instructions, "filing checklist," and the Articles of Organization fill-in-the-blank form.

WHAT MUST BE FILED:

The original and one copy of the Articles of Organization must be filed with the Corporation Commission, copies will be returned if all requirements have been satisfied. DOMESTIC companies must publish a Notice of Filing: Within sixty days after filing, three consecutive publications of the Articles of Organization must be published in a newspaper of general circulation where the LLC has its place of business. Within ninety days after filing, an Affidavit evidencing the publication must also be filed with the Commission. This Affidavit will be supplied by the newspaper.

NAME REQUIREMENTS:

The name must contain the words "Limited Liability Company" or the abbreviations "L.L.C." or "L.C." You should check with the LLC filing office if the desired name is available. A name can be reserved for 120 days for a fee of $10. If you're a holder of a tradename or trademark that is identical or non-distinguishable from the proposed name, make sure you have a copy of the tradename certificate to attach to the Articles of Organization.

ARTICLES SPECIAL REQUIREMENTS:

The LLC must have a registered office and a statutory agent at a street address. The agent must sign the Articles or provide a consent to acceptance of appointment.

FILING FEES:

There is a $50 filing fee for Domestic LLCs and $150 for Foreign LLCs. Also, an expedited service is available for an additional $35 fee. Fees must be paid to the "Arizona Corporation Commission."

REPORTS:

Like a domestic corporation, the LLC must deliver to the commission for filing an annual report containing the basic information about the company and its financial condition. The annual filing fee is to be paid on or before the date assigned by the commission.

RECORDS REQUIRED:

- Names and addresses of members and managers
- Articles and all amendments
- Three years of financial records
- Three years of tax returns
- Operating agreement and all amendments

STATUTES:

Title 29, Chapter 4, Arizona Statutes (Arizona Limited Liability Company Act).

ARKANSAS

Secretary of State
Corporation Division
State Capitol
Little Rock, AR 72201-1094
501-682-3409

Website: www.sosweb.state.ar.us

State sends material within ten days.

WHAT THEY SUPPLY:

State provides duplicate of fill-in-the-blank Articles of Organization form with instructions and an application for the franchise tax reporting form.

WHAT MUST BE FILED:

File two copies of Articles of Organization. A file stamped copy will be returned to you after filing has been completed. Also file one copy of Limited Liability Company Franchise Tax registration form.

NAME REQUIREMENTS:

The name must contain the words "Limited Liability Company" or the abbreviation "L.L.C.," "L.C.," "LLC," or "LC." Companies which perform Professional Service must additionally contain the words "Professional Limited Liability Company," or the abbreviations "P.L.L.C.," "P.L.C.," "PLLC," or "PLC."

An LLC name may be reserved for 120 days for a fee of $25.

ARTICLES SPECIAL REQUIREMENTS:

Registered agent must sign acknowledgement and acceptance of the appointment.

If the management of the company is vested in managers this must be stated in the articles.

FILING FEES:

There is a $50 filing fee for domestic companies, $300 for foreign LLCs.

REPORTS:

The annual report is due before June 1 each year. The filing fee is $109.

RECORDS REQUIRED:

- Names and addresses of members and managers
- Articles and all amendments
- Three years of financial records
- Three years of tax returns
- Operating agreement and all amendments

STATUTES:

Small Business Entity Tax Pass Through Act, Act 1003 of 1993, Ark. Code Annotated, beginning with Section 4-32-101.

CALIFORNIA

Office of the Secretary of State
Limited Liability Company Unit
1500 - 11th Street, 3rd Floor
P.O. Box 944228
Sacramento, CA 94244-2250
916-653-3365

Website: www.ss.ca.gov/business/business.htm

State sends material within ten days.

WHAT THEY SUPPLY:

State provides any fill-in-the-blank forms concerning the limited liability company with instructions and a fee schedule.

WHAT MUST BE FILED:

File only the original executed document together with the filing fee. A certified copy of the original document will be returned to you after filing.

NAME REQUIREMENTS:

The name must end with the words "limited liability company", "Ltd. Liability Co." or the abbreviation "LLC," or "L.L.C." as the last words. It must not be similar to a name of any other existing limited liability company. It may contain the name of one or two members, but may not contain the words "bank," "insurance," "trust," "corporation," or "incorporated."

For name reservation, file an application with the secretary of state with a $10 fee. If the desired name is available it will be reserved for a period of sixty days.

In California, you *can't* form a professional limited liability company.

MEMBERS REQUIREMENTS:

Single member limited liability companies may now be formed.

ARTICLES SPECIAL REQUIREMENTS:

The Articles must be filed on California form LLC-1 and not a substitute. A form is on the next page.

FILING FEES:

There is a filing fee of $70, payable to the "Limited Liability Company Unit." However, see the other fees below.

REPORTS:

The annual minimum tax for "the privilege of doing business in California" is $800. You must pay this fee within three months after forming your LLC. If the total income of your LLC is more than $249,999, there's an additional fee of $500 and if it is over 499,999 the fee goes up in steps to $4,500 annually.

A tax voucher (form 3522) must be requested from the Franchise Tax Board. The toll-free number is 800-852-5711.

RECORDS REQUIRED:

- Names and addresses of members and managers
- Articles and all amendments
- Three years of financial records
- Six years of tax returns
- Operating agreement and all amendments

STATUTES:

California Corporation Code, Section 17000-17062 (Beverly-Killea Limited Liability Company Act).

State of California
Kevin Shelley
Secretary of State

LIMITED LIABILITY COMPANY
ARTICLES OF ORGANIZATION

A $70.00 filing fee must accompany this form.
IMPORTANT – Read instructions before completing this form.

File#_____

This Space For Filing Use Only

---

1. Name of the limited liability company (end the name with the words "Limited Liability Company," " Ltd. Liability Co.," or the abbreviations "LLC" or "L.L.C.")

---

2. The purpose of the limited liability company is to engage in any lawful act or activity for which a limited liability company may be organized under the Beverly-Killea limited liability company act.

---

3. Name the agent for service of process and check the appropriate provision below:

_____ which is

[ ] an individual residing in California. Proceed to item 4.

[ ] a corporation which has filed a certificate pursuant to section 1505. Proceed to item 5.

---

4. If an individual, California address of the agent for service of process:
   Address:

   City: State: **CA**   Zip Code:

---

5. The limited liability company will be managed by: **(check one)**

[ ] one manager   [ ] more than one manager   [ ] single member limited liability company   [ ] all limited liability company members

---

6. Other matters to be included in this certificate may be set forth on separate attached pages and are made a part of this certificate. Other matters may include the latest date on which the limited liability company is to dissolve.

---

7. Number of pages attached, if any:

---

8. Type of business of the limited liability company. (For informational purposes only)

---

9. **DECLARATION:** It is hereby declared that I am the person who executed this instrument, which execution is my act and deed.

   _____   _____
   Signature of Organizer   Type or Print Name of Organizer

   _____
   Date

---

10. **RETURN TO:**

    NAME

    FIRM

    ADDRESS

    CITY/STATE

    ZIP CODE

SEC/STATE (REV. 01/03)

FORM LLC-1 – FILING FEE $70.00
Approved by Secretary of State

78

INSTRUCTIONS FOR COMPLETING THE ARTICLES OF ORGANIZATION (LLC-1)

DO NOT ALTER THIS FORM

Type or legibly print in black ink.

Pursuant to California Corporation Code Section 17375, nothing in this title shall be construed to permit a domestic or foreign limited liability company to render professional services, as defined in subdivision (a) of Section 13401, in this state.

- Attach the fee for filing the Articles of Organization (LLC-1) with the Secretary of State. The fee is seventy dollars ($70).

- Make check(s) payable to the Secretary of State.

- Send the executed document and filing fee to:

  California Secretary of State
  Limited Liability Company Unit
  P.O. Box 944228
  Sacramento, CA 94244-2280

- Fill in the items as follows:

Item 1. Enter the name of the limited liability company. The name shall contain the words "Limited Liability Company," or the abbreviations "LLC" or "L.L.C." The words "Limited" and "Company" may be abbreviated to "Ltd." and "Co." The name of the limited liability company may not contain the words "bank," "trust," "trustee," incorporated," "inc.," "corporation," or "corp.," and shall not contain the words "insurer" or "insurance company" or any other words suggesting that it is in the business of issuing policies of insurance and assuming insurance risks. (Section 17052)

Item 2. Execution of this document confirms the following statement which has been preprinted on the form and may not be altered: "The purpose of the limited liability company is to engage in any lawful act or activity for which a limited liability company may be organized under the Beverly-Killea Limited Liability Company Act." Provisions limiting or restricting the business of the limited liability company may be included as an attachment.

Item 3. Enter the name of the agent for service of process. Check the appropriate provision indicating whether the agent is an individual residing in California or a corporation which has filed a certificate pursuant to Section 1505 of the California Corporations Code. If an individual is designated as agent, proceed to item 4. If a corporation is designated, proceed to item 5.

Item 4. If an individual is designated as the initial agent for service of process, enter an address in California. Do not enter "in care of" (c/o) or abbreviate the name of the city. DO NOT enter an address if a corporation is designated as the agent for service of process.

Item 5. Check the appropriate provision indicating whether the limited liability company is to be managed by one manager, more than one manager, single member limited liability company or the all limited liability company members. Section 17051(a)(5).

Item 6. The Articles of Organization (LLC-1) may include other matters that the person filing the Articles of Organization determines to include. Other matters may include the latest date on which the limited liability company is to dissolve. If other matters are to be included, attach one or more pages setting forth the other matters.

Item 7. Enter the number of pages attached, if any. All attachments should be 8½" x 11", one-sided and legible.

Item 8. Briefly describe the type of business that constitutes the principal business activity of the limited liability company. Note restrictions in the rendering of professional services by Limited Liability Companies. Professional services are defined in California Corporations Code, Section 13401(a) as: "Any type of professional services that may be lawfully rendered only pursuant to a license, certification, or registration authorized by the Business and Professions Code or the Chiropractic Act."

Item 9. **Declaration:** The Articles of Organization (LLC-1) shall be executed with an original signature of the organizer. A facsimile or photocopy of the signature is not acceptable for the purpose of filing with the Secretary of State.

The person executing the Articles of Organization (LLC-1) need not be a member or manager of the limited liability company.

If an entity is signing the Articles of Organization (LLC-1), the person who signs for the entity must note the exact entity name, his/her name, and his/her position/title.

If an attorney-in-fact is signing the Articles of Organization (LLC-1), the signature must be followed by the words "Attorney-in-fact for (name of person)."

If a trust is signing the Articles of Organization (LLC-1), the articles must be signed by a trustee as follows: _____, trustee for_____trust (including the date of the trust, if applicable). Example: Mary Todd, trustee of the Lincoln Family Trust (U/T/A 5-1-94).

Item 10. **Enter the name and the address of the person or firm to whom a copy of the filing should be returned.**

- Statutory provisions can be found in Section 17051 of the California Corporations Code, unless otherwise indicated.

- For further information contact the Limited Liability Company Unit at (916) 653-3795.

COLORADO

Secretary of State
Corporations Office
1560 Broadway, Suite 200
Denver, CO 80202
303-894-2251

Website:
www.state.co.us/pubs/business/main.htm

State sends material within two weeks.

WHAT THEY SUPPLY:

State provides single copy of fill-in-the-blank Articles of Organization form.

WHAT MUST BE FILED:

You must file the typed original and one copy of the Articles of Organization with the secretary of state. You need to include a self-addressed envelope.

NAME REQUIREMENTS:

The name must contain the words "Limited Liability Company" or the abbreviation "LLC" or "L.L.C." The word "Limited" may be abbreviated as "Ltd." the word company as "Co."

You can check name availability by calling the secretary of state. A name reservation can be made for a $10 fee for 120 days.

ARTICLES SPECIAL REQUIREMENTS:

No special requirements.

FILING FEES:

There is a fee of $50 for the regular filing (payable to the "Secretary of State"), an additional $50 is required for expedited service (filing within twenty-four hours).

REPORTS:

Every two years a report must be filed with a $25 fee.

RECORDS REQUIRED:

- Names and addresses of members and managers
- Articles and all amendments
- Three years of financial records
- Three years of tax returns
- Operating agreement and all amendments
- Minutes of meetings
- Members' contributions
- Members' right of termination

STATUTES:

Colorado Limited Liability Company Act, Colorado Revised Statutes, beginning with Section 7-80-101.

CONNECTICUT ·

Secretary of State
30 Trinity Street
P.O. Box 150470
Hartford, CT 06106-0470
860-509-6079

Website:
www.sots.state.ct.us/Business/BusinessMain.html

WHAT THEY SUPPLY:

State provides fill-in-the-blank Articles of Organization form with instructions.

WHAT MUST BE FILED:

Single copy of Articles of Organization must be filed with the secretary of state. You will receive a mailing receipt. Copies are at additional charge (see below).

NAME REQUIREMENTS:

The name must contain the words "Limited Liability Company" or the abbreviation "L.L.C." The words "Limited" and "Company" may be abbreviated as "Ltd." and "Co."

For name availability check with the secretary of state. A name reservation can be made for 120 days for a fee of $30.

ARTICLES SPECIAL REQUIREMENTS:

Statutory agent must sign.

FILING FEES:

There is a filing fee of $60, payable to the "Secretary of State." For a certified copy add an extra $25 for each document. For an ordinary copy the fee is $20.

REPORTS:

Annual report required with fee of $10.

RECORDS REQUIRED:

- Names and addresses of members and managers
- Articles and all amendments
- Three years of financial records
- Three years of tax returns
- Operating agreement and all amendments
- Names of past members and managers
- Prior operating agreements
- Members' contributions
- Members' right of termination

STATUTES:

Connecticut Limited Liability Company Act, Pub. Act 93-267, Connecticut Statutes, Title 34.

DELAWARE

State of Delaware
Division of Corporations
John G. Townsend Building
401 Federal Street, Suite 4
Dover, DE 19901
302-739-3073
Name Reservation: 900-420-8042

Website: www.state.de.us/corp.htm

State sends material within two weeks.

WHAT THEY SUPPLY:

State provides complete booklet about how to form a business in Delaware. This contains fill-in-the-blank Certificate of Formation, fee schedules, a franchise tax schedule, phone and fax directory, a list of registered agents and other important information.

WHAT MUST BE FILED:

The original and one copy of the Certificate of Formation must be filed with the secretary of state. The documents must be submitted in the U.S. letter size (8.5"x11") with certain margins and must be either typed, printed or written in black ink.

NAME REQUIREMENTS:

The name must contain the words "Limited Liability Company" or the abbreviation "L.L.C."

A name can be reserved for 120 days for a fee of $75.

ARTICLES SPECIAL REQUIREMENTS:

The document is called a "Certificate of Formation" in Delaware and has only three requirements, the name, address of the registered office and name of registered agent.

FILING FEES:

The initial filing fee is $50, payable to the "Division of Corporations." Certified copies can be received for an additional $20 each. The Corporations' Division accepts major credit cards.

REPORTS:

Annual reports are required with a filing fee of $100 by June 1.

RECORDS REQUIRED:

- None required by statute.

STATUTES:

Title 6, Commerce and Trade, Chapter 18, Limited Liability Company Act.

DISTRICT OF COLUMBIA

Department of Consumer and Regulatory Affairs
Corporation Division
941 North Capital Street N.E.
Washington, D.C. 20002
202-442-4432

Website:
www.dcra.dc.gov/information/build_pla
/business_services/corporations_division.shtm

State sends materials within ten days.

WHAT THEY SUPPLY:

Office provides a sample of Articles of Organization (but no forms) with instructions on how to draft your own document. A blank form of a written consent of the registered agent is included.

WHAT MUST BE FILED:

You must file two signed originals of Articles of Organization. Attach the written consent of the registered agent.

NAME REQUIREMENTS:

The name must contain the words "Limited Liability Company" or the abbreviation "L.L.C." A name may be reserved for sixty days for $25. If your company is going to perform professional service, the name must contain the words "Professional Limited Liability Company."

ARTICLES SPECIAL REQUIREMENTS:

The registered agent must consent to his appointment.

If a general or limited partnership converts to a limited liability company, the former name and fact of conversion must be stated Articles of Organization.

FILING FEES:

There is a filing fee of $100 for a domestic LLC, payable to the "D.C. Treasurer."

REPORTS:

Annual report due every other year by June 16th, starting the first year after organizing, with $100 fee.

RECORDS REQUIRED:

- Names and addresses of members and managers
- Articles and all amendments
- Three years of financial records
- Three years of tax returns
- Operating agreement and all amendments

STATUTES:

Title 29, Chapter 10 of the District of Columbia Code (D.C. Limited Liability Company Act of 1994).

FLORIDA

Secretary of State
Division of Corporations
P.O. Box 6327
Tallahassee, FL 32314
850-488-9000

Website: www.dos.state.fl.us

State sends material within one week.

WHAT THEY SUPPLY:

State provides complete filing package, including a booklet "Florida Limited Liability Company Act," a "Fictitious Name Registration Packet," a fill-in-the-blank Articles of Organization form and complete instructions.

WHAT MUST BE FILED:

unless this material has been included in your articles, one original copy of the Articles of Organization must be filed along with the Certificate of Designation of Registered Agent. An Affidavit of Membership and Contributions must also be filed unless this information is included in your articles. If you include a copy of the articles, it will be date-stamped and returned. Otherwise, you will receive an acknowledgement letter.

NAME REQUIREMENTS:

The company name must end with the words "Limited Liability Company" or "Limited Company" or the abbreviation "L.L.C." or "L.C." The name may not contain language implying that the LLC is connected with a state or federal government agency. It must be distinguishable from other company names already on file.

For name availability, check the Florida Website: (www.dos.state.fl.us).

ARTICLES SPECIAL REQUIREMENTS:

If the Limited Liability Company is to be managed by one or more managers, a statement that the company is to be a manager-managed company needs to be included in the Articles.

An acceptance by the registered agent and an affidavit of membership and contributions must be either included in the Articles or on a separate form.

FILING FEES:

There is a filing fee of $100 for the Articles of Organization and the Affidavit plus an additional $25 for the Certificate of Designation of the registered agent. For another (optional) fee of $30, you can get a certified copy of the Articles. Make the check with the minimum fee ($125) payable to the "Florida Department of State."

REPORTS:

An annual report must be filed between January 1 and May 1 of each year with the annual fee of $50. If you fail to file the annual report in time, there's a $400 late fee!

RECORDS REQUIRED:

- Names and addresses of members
- Articles and all amendments
- Three years of financial records
- Three years of tax returns
- Operating agreement and all amendments
- Members' contributions

STATUTES:

Title 36, Chapter 608, Florida Statutes (Florida Limited Liability Company Act).

NOTE: *As this books goes to press, major revisions of the Florida Act are pending before the legislature.*

Georgia

Secretary of State
2 Martin Luther King, Jr. Drive
Suite 315, West Tower
Atlanta, GA 30334-1530
404-656-2817

Website: www.sos.state.ga.us/corporations

State sends materials within two weeks.

WHAT THEY SUPPLY:

State provides instructions for filing self-drafted Articles of Organization and gives a sample form containing the minimum of two articles. Also a Transmittal Form is provided which must be filed with the Articles of Organization.

WHAT MUST BE FILED:

You must file the original and one copy of the Articles of Organization and attach the Transmittal form provided by the State.

NAME REQUIREMENTS:

The name must contain the words "Limited Liability Company" or "Limited Company" or the abbreviation "L.L.C." or "LLC."

A name should be reserved prior to filing. The reservation can be made at the website, **www.georgiacorporations.org**, or by faxing a request to (404) 651-7842. Reservations are not available by telephone.

If your proposed name is available, you'll be mailed a reservation certificate with a reservation number that remains in effect for ninety days. The reservation number must be placed in the Transmittal Form that is filed with your Articles of Organization.

ARTICLES SPECIAL REQUIREMENTS:

The name of the company must be in the Articles. If the company is to be managed by someone other than the members, a clause should be added indicating who are the managers. Other information, such as the address of the company and registered agent, is to be included on the "Transmittal Information" sheet.

The Articles must be signed by all members.

FILING FEES:

There is a filing fee of $75, payable to the "Secretary of State."

REPORTS:

Annual report due before April 1 with $25 filing fee.

RECORDS REQUIRED:

- Names and addresses of members and managers
- Articles and all amendments
- Three years of financial records
- Three years of tax returns
- Operating agreement and all amendments

STATUTES:

Title 14, Chapter 11 of the Official Code of Georgia Annotated.

Hawaii

Business Registration Division
Department of Commerce
and Consumer Affairs
1010 Richards Street
P.O. Box 40
Honolulu, HI 96810
808-586-2744

Website: www.businessregistrations.com

WHAT THEY SUPPLY:

State provides instructions and blank forms.

WHAT MUST BE FILED:

You must file the original and one copy of the Articles of Organization.

NAME REQUIREMENTS:

The name must contain the words "Limited Liability Company" or "Limited Company" or the abbreviation "L.L.C." or "LLC."

The abbreviations "Ltd." and "Co." can be used.

ARTICLES SPECIAL REQUIREMENTS:

The Articles should state that the members are not liable for the debts of the company under Section 428-303(c) Hawaii Statutes.

If there are managers their names and residence addresses must be included, otherwise the name and residence addresses of the members must be listed.

FILING FEES:

There is a filing fee of $100, payable to the "Department of Commerce and Consumer Affairs." Reviewing time is approximately twenty-two days unless you pay an additional $50.

REPORTS:

Annual report with $25 filing fee. The report is due before June 30 every year. The forms will be mailed to you before that date.

RECORDS REQUIRED:

- Names and addresses of members and managers
- Articles and all amendments
- Three years of financial records
- Three years of tax returns
- Operating agreement and all amendments
- Past members and managers

STATUTES:

Title 23A, Chapter 428, Hawaii Revised Statutes.

IDAHO

Secretary of State
700 W. Jefferson, Room 203
Boise, ID 83720-0080
208-334-2300

Website: www.idsos.state.id.us/

State sends material within one week.

WHAT THEY SUPPLY:

State provides two fill-in-the-blank Articles of Organization forms with instructions and, on request, a booklet containing the Limited Liability Company Act.

WHAT MUST BE FILED:

You must file two completed originals. The fill-in-the-blank forms must be typed, if not typed or if the attachments are not included, there's an additional $20 fee for filing.

If you have questions about the correct filing, you can call the secretary of state's office at 208-334-2301.

NAME REQUIREMENTS:

The name must contain the words "Limited Liability Company" or the abbreviation "L.L.C." or "L.C." The word "Limited" may be abbreviated as "Ltd.," and the word "Company" as "Co."

If you want to perform professional services, the company's name must end with the words "Professional Company" or the abbreviation "P.L.L.C." or "PLLC."

A name may be reserved for $20 for four months.

ARTICLES SPECIAL REQUIREMENTS:

The address of the registered office may not be a P.O. Box, but must be a physical address in Idaho. The registered agent must sign the articles. If the management shall be vested in managers, at least one manager has to sign the Articles.

The name and address of at least one manager or member must be included.

FILING FEES:

There is a filing fee of $100, payable to the "Idaho Secretary of State." If the articles are not typed or if there are attachments, there is an additional $20 fee. Expedited service is an additional $20.

REPORTS:

The annnual report shall be delivered to the secretary of state each year before the end of the month during which your company was initially organized, beginning one year after it is organized.

RECORDS REQUIRED:

- Names and addresses of members and managers
- Articles and all amendments
- Three years of financial records
- Three years of tax returns
- Operating agreement and all amendments
- Past members and managers

STATUTES:

Title 53, Chapter 6, Idaho Limited Liability Company Act.

ILLINOIS

Secretary of State
Business Services Dept.
501 South Second Street
Room 359, Howlett Building
Springfield, IL 62756
217-782-6961

Website:
www.sos.state.il.us/departments/business_services
/business.html

State sends materials within three weeks.

WHAT THEY SUPPLY:

State provides complete filing package, including numerous forms, booklets "The Illinois Limited Liability Company Act" and "Limited Liability Corporations," a name fee schedule, phone directory and a Business Activity Code which is similar to the Standard Industrial Code (SIC).

WHAT MUST BE FILED:

File the original and one copy of the signed Articles of Organization form. The form must be typed.

NAME REQUIREMENTS:

The company's name must contain the words "Limited Liability Company," "L.L.C.," or "LLC," but may not contain the terms "Ltd.," "Co.," "Inc.," "Corporation," "Corp.," "Incorporated," "Partnership," or "LP." It must be distinguishable from other company names already on file.

A name may be reserved using a special Reservation form (included in the filing package) for a $300 (!) fee. We suggest to just check the name availability under 217-782-9520 if a reservation is not essential.

ARTICLES SPECIAL REQUIREMENTS:

If there are managers, their names and residence addresses must be included; otherwise the name and residence addresses of the members must be listed.

In Article 6 you are asked for the business purpose by (SIC) code. However, the statute states that the purpose can be "any or all lawful business."

FILING FEES:

The fee is $400, and must be made by a certified check, cashier's check, Illinois attorney's check, or money order, payable to "Secretary of State."

REPORTS:

The annual report must be delivered to the secretary of state before the first day of the anniversary month. The annual fee is $200. If you fail to file the report within another sixty day period after the first day of the anniversary month, there will be a penalty of $100.

RECORDS REQUIRED:

- Names, addresses and dates of members
- Articles and all amendments
- Three years of financial records
- Three years of tax returns
- Operating agreement and all amendments
- Members' contributions

STATUTES:

The Illinois Limited Liability Company Act, 805 ILCS 180.

INDIANA

Secretary of State
302 W. Washington, Room E018
Indianapolis, IN 46204
317-232-6576

Website: www.state.in.us/sos

WHAT THEY SUPPLY:

State provides instructions how to draft your own Articles of Organization, it also includes a fee schedule and instructions on how to download forms from their website.

WHAT MUST BE FILED:

File original and two copies of the Articles of Organization with the secretary of state. Enclose the filing fee.

NAME REQUIREMENTS:

The company name must contain the words "limited liability company," "L.L.C.," or "LLC." It must be distinguishable from other companies already on file. You can get a name reservation for 120 days for a $20 fee. For availability, you can check by phone.

ARTICLES SPECIAL REQUIREMENTS:

No unusual clauses are required.

FILING FEES:

There is a filing fee of $90, payable to the "Secretary of State."

REPORTS:

Annual report must be filed with $30 filing fee. The report is due in the anniversary month of the company every two years. If your company was organized in an odd year, you need to report every odd year, and if it was organized in an even year, your report needs to be filed every even year.

RECORDS REQUIRED:

- Names and addresses of members and managers
- Articles and all amendments
- Three years of financial records
- Three years of tax returns
- Operating agreement and all amendments

STATUTES:

Indiana Code Title 23, Chapter 18.

IOWA

Secretary of State
Corporations Division
Lucas Building, 1st Floor
321 E. 12th Street
Des Moines, IA 50319
515-281-5204

Website: www.sos.state.ia.us/

WHAT THEY SUPPLY:

State provides a copy of the law, but no forms. In section 490A.303, you'll find the requirements for the Articles of Organization.

WHAT MUST BE FILED:

File only the original of your Articles of Organization. The document must be typed or printed in black ink. If all requirements are met, the Articles will be returned as filed.

NAME REQUIREMENTS:

The company name must contain the words "Limited Company" or the abbreviation " L.C.," but may not contain the words "Corporation," "Incorporated," "Corp." or the like. It must be distinguishable from company names already on file.

For a $10 fee you can reserve a name for 120 days.

ARTICLES SPECIAL REQUIREMENTS:

The principal office must be listed. (This may be the same as the registered office, but doesn't need to be.)

FILING FEES:

There is a filing fee of $50, payable to the "Secretary of State."

REPORTS:

No annual reporting fee.

RECORDS REQUIRED:

- Names and addresses of members and managers
- Articles and all amendments
- Three years of financial records
- Three years of tax returns
- Operating agreement and all amendments

STATUTES:

Chapter 490A, Iowa Codes, Iowa Limited Liability Company Act.

KANSAS

Secretary of State
Corporation Division
1st Floor, Memorial Hall
120 SW 10th Avenue
Topeka, KS 66612-1594
785-296-4564

Website: www.state.ks.us/public/sos/

State sends material within one week.

WHAT THEY SUPPLY:

State provides one copy of fill-in-the-blank Articles of Organization with instructions.

WHAT MUST BE FILED:

The Articles of Organization must be signed by the person forming the organization or by any member or manager. You must file the original signed copy and one duplicate, which may either be a signed or conformed copy. Enclose the filing fee.

NAME REQUIREMENTS:

The company name must contain the words "limited company" or the abbreviations "L.C." or "LC," or the words "Limited Liability Company" or the abbreviations "L.L.C." or "LLC." The name must be distinguishable from other entity names in Kansas.

ARTICLES SPECIAL REQUIREMENTS:

The address of its registered office and the address of the registered agent for service of process must be the same, but the agent can be the LLC itself.

If the members have the right to admit additional members, this must be included in the articles along with the terms and conditions of the admission.

If the remaining members have the right to continue the business upon any event which terminates the continued membership of a member of the limited liability company, this must be included.

The names and addresses of the managers or if none, names and addresses of the members must be included.

FILING FEES:

There is a filing fee of $150, payable to the "Secretary of State."

REPORTS:

Annual report with a minimum of $25 fee. The report is due the fifteenth day of the fourth month following the close of your company's fiscal year.

RECORDS REQUIRED:

- Names and addresses of members and managers
- Articles and all amendments
- Three years of financial records
- Three years of tax returns
- Minutes and resolutions

STATUTES:

Kansas Statutes Annotated, beginning with Section 17-7601.

KENTUCKY

Commonwealth of Kentucky
Office of the Secretary of State
Capitol Building, Room 152
Frankfort, KY 40601
502-564-2848

Website: www.sos.state.ky.us

State sends material within one week.

WHAT THEY SUPPLY:

State provides fill-in-the-blank Articles of Organization and filing instructions.

WHAT MUST BE FILED:

File your typewritten (or printed) and signed Articles original accompanied by two exact copies. If the company will be managed by managers, the documents must be signed by the managers, or by a least one member. The person signing the document has to state the capacity in which she or he signs.

NAME REQUIREMENTS:

The name must contain the words "Limited Liability Company," or "Limited Company," or the abbreviations "LLC" or "LC." The word "Limited" may be abbreviated as "Ltd." and the word "Company" as "Co."

Professional LLCs must contain the words "Professional Limited Company" or "Professional Limited Liability Company" or the abbreviation "PLLC" or "PLC."

The name must be distinguishable from any other name on record with the secretary of state. You can check the name availability by calling 502-564-2848. A name can be reserved for a $15 fee for a period of 120 days.

ARTICLES SPECIAL REQUIREMENTS:

The registered agent must consent to his or her appointment by signing the articles.

FILING FEES:

There is a filing fee of $40 payable to the "Kentucky State Treasurer."

REPORTS:

The first annual report must be delivered to the secretary of state between January 1 and June 30 of the year following the calendar year in which the company was organized. Reports are due June 30 in each subsequent year. The annual fee is $15.

RECORDS REQUIRED:

- Names and addresses of members and managers
- Articles and all amendments
- Three years of financial records
- Three years of tax returns
- Operating agreement and all amendments

STATUTES:

Chapter 275 Kentucky Statutes, Kentucky Limited Liability Company Act.

LOUISIANA

Secretary of State
Corporations Division
P.O. Box 94125
Baton Rouge, LA 70804-9125
225-925-4704

Website: www.sec.state.la.us/

State sends material within one week.

WHAT THEY SUPPLY:

State provides fill-in-the-blank Articles of Organization and a "Limited Liability Company Initial Report" that contains the agent's affidavit and acknowledgment of acceptance. Both forms come with instructions. For a fee of $10, you can receive a "Corporation Laws" booklet which covers LLC laws.

WHAT MUST BE FILED:

Complete both the Articles and the Initial Report. Both documents must be signed by the people organizing the LLC and both must be notarized. File only the originals and enclose the filing fee.

NAME REQUIREMENTS:

Your company name must contain the words "Limited Liability Company" or the abbreviation "L.L.C." or "L.C."

Names can be reserved for a fee of $20 for sixty days.

ARTICLES SPECIAL REQUIREMENTS:

Articles of Organization must be notarized. They must be accompanied by form 973 "Initial Report" which must be signed by all persons who signed the Articles of Organization and the registered agent and be notarized.

FILING FEES:

There is a filing fee of $60, payable to the "Secretary of State."

REPORTS:

Annual report required with $25 filing fee. The report is due on the anniversary date of the organization. The forms will be mailed to you one month prior to the due date.

RECORDS REQUIRED:

- Names and addresses of members and managers
- Articles and all amendments
- Three years of financial records
- Three years of tax returns
- Operating agreement and all amendments

STATUTES:

Louisiana Revised Statutes beginning with Section 12:1301.

MAINE

Secretary of State
Bureau of Corporations, Elections, and
Commissions
101 State House Station
Augusta, ME 04333-0101
207-624-7736

Website: www.state.me.us/sos/sos.htm

State sends material within ten days.

WHAT THEY SUPPLY:

State provides blank forms for Articles of
Organization and Acceptance of Appointment as
Registered Agent. State also provides general information on the different types of business entities,
including the LLC.

WHAT MUST BE FILED:

File the typewritten or printed original Articles of
Organization. If the registered agent does not sign the
Articles, he or she must sign the Acceptance of
Appointment as Registered Agent.

NAME REQUIREMENTS:

The name must contain the words "Limited Liability
Company," "L.L.C." or "LLC."

A Professional LLC must contain the words
"Chartered," "Professional Association" or the
abbreviation "P.A."

You can reserve a name by filing the application form
with a $20 fee.

ARTICLES SPECIAL REQUIREMENTS:

If there are managers, a statement to that effect must
be included along with the minimum and maximum
number of managers. If they have been selected, their
names and addresses must be included.

FILING FEES:

There is a filing fee of $125 payable to the Secretary
of State.

REPORTS:

Annual report required with $60 filing fee.

RECORDS REQUIRED:

- Names and addresses of members and managers
- Articles and all amendments
- Operating agreement and all amendments
- Past members and managers

STATUTES:

Maine Revised Statutes Title 31, Chapter 13, beginning
with Section 601-762.

MARYLAND

State Department of Assessments and Taxation
Corporate Charter Division
301 West Preston Street, Room 801
Baltimore, MD 21202-2395
410-767-1184

Website: www.sos.state.md.us

WHAT THEY SUPPLY:

State provides instructions on how to draft your Articles of Organization and a fill-in-the-blank form of Articles.

WHAT MUST BE FILED:

Type or print your Articles, handwritten documents are not accepted. Submit the signed original for filing. If you want a certified copy, add an additional $6 plus $1 to your filing check for each additional page.

NAME REQUIREMENTS:

The company name must contain the words "Limited Liability Company," or one of the following abbreviations: "L.L.C.," "LLC," "L.C.," or "LC."

For the name availability, please check with the secretary of state at 410-767-1340. A name reservation can be made for a $7 fee.

ARTICLES SPECIAL REQUIREMENTS:

No special items are required in the Articles, but they request that the return address of the Articles be clearly noted.

FILING FEES:

There is a filing fee of $50, payable to the "State Department of Assessments & Taxation."

REPORTS:

Report must be filed every five years with filing fee of $50.

RECORDS REQUIRED:

- Names and addresses of members and managers
- Articles and all amendments
- Three years of financial records
- Three years of tax returns
- Operating agreement and all amendments

STATUTES:

Maryland Code, Corps. & Ass'ns., beginning with Section 4A-101.

MASSACHUSETTS

Secretary of the Commonwealth
Corporations Division
One Ashburton Place, 17th Floor
Boston, MA 02108
617-727-9640 or 617-727-2850

Website:
www.state.ma.us/sec/cor/coridx.htm

State sends material within one week.

WHAT THEY SUPPLY:

State provides printed copies of its website. It provides instructions, how to draft your own Certificate of Organization, and general information on LLCs.

WHAT MUST BE FILED:

File the original signed copy together with a photocopy or a duplicate original. The documents must be signed either by the person forming the LLC, by any manager (if there are any), or by a trustee.

NAME REQUIREMENTS:

The company name must contain the words "Limited Liability Company," "Limited Company," or the abbreviation "L.L.C.," "L.C.," "LLC" or " LC."

It must be distinguishable from any other company name on record. You can reserve a name for thirty days by filing an application with the Division specifying the name to be reserved and the name and address of the applicant. The reservation fee is $15.

ARTICLES SPECIAL REQUIREMENTS:

If available, the Federal Employer Identification Number (FEIN) should be included on the articles. This is obtained by filing IRS form SS-4 (form 3 in appendix C). If the number is needed quickly it can be obtained over the phone (404-455-2360), but you must have form SS-4 completed and in front of you.

If there are managers, their names and residence addresses must be included. If the managers' business addresses are different from that of the LLC, their addresses must be listed.

If there is anyone other than a manager who is authorized to execute papers filed with the Corporations Division, their name and business must be included. If there are no managers, at least one member's name and business address must be listed.

FILING FEES:

There is a filing fee of $500, payable to the "Commonwealth of Massachusetts."

REPORTS:

An annual report must be filed on or before the anniversary date of the filing of its original certificate or organization. The report must contain all information required for the certificate, the annual fee is $500.

RECORDS REQUIRED:

- Names and addresses of members
- Articles and all amendments
- Three years of financial records
- Three years of tax returns
- Operating agreement and all amendments

STATUTES:

Annotated Laws of massachusetts, Title 22, Chapter 156C, Massachusetts Limited Liability Act.

MICHIGAN

Michigan Department of Commerce
Corporation and Securities Bureau
Corporation Division
P.O. Box 30054
Lansing, MI 48909-7554
517-241-6470

Website:
www.michigan.gov/emi
/0,1303,7-102-115-,00.html

State sends material within ten days.

WHAT THEY SUPPLY:

The Filing Office sends you fill-in-the-blank Articles of Organization.

WHAT MUST BE FILED:

The Articles must be typed or filled in with black ink. Either form C&S 700 must be used for the Articles or it should accompany your Articles.

If you prefer the fax filing procedure, fill in the "ELF Application" form (you must provide your Visa/Mastercard number here), the cover sheet and check the fax filing checklist (provided by the State).

NAME REQUIREMENTS:

The company name must contain the words "Limited Liability Company," or the abbreviation "L.L.C.," "LLC," "L.C.," or "LC." If you want to perform professional services, the name must contain the words "Professional Limited Liability Company," or the abbreviation "P.L.L.C." or "P.L.C."

For name availability, call 517-241-6470. You can make a reservation for a period of six months for a fee of $25. Use the Application form provided by the state.

ARTICLES SPECIAL REQUIREMENTS:

The Articles of Organization must be either on form C&S 700 (which has specific spaces for filing number, date received and return address) or a "comparable document." If you have drafted your own articles, they suggest that you attach C&S 700 as a cover sheet.

FILING FEES:

There is a $50 nonrefundable fee, payable to the "State of Michigan."

REPORTS:

Annual report required with $10 filing fee.

RECORDS REQUIRED:

- Names and addresses of members and managers
- Articles and all amendments
- Three years of financial records
- Three years of tax returns
- Operating agreement and all amendments
- Voting rights
- Terms for distributions

STATUTES:

Act 23 of the Public Acts of 1993, Michigan Limited Liability Company Act, or Michigan Compiled Laws, beginning with Section 450.4101.

MINNESOTA

Secretary of State
Division of Corporations
180 State Office Building
100 Constitution Avenue
St. Paul, MN 55155-1299
612-296-2803

Website:
www.sos.state.mn.us/business/index.html

State sends material within two weeks.

WHAT THEY SUPPLY:

State provides one-page fill-in-the-blank Articles of Organization with instructions.

WHAT MUST BE FILED:

Type or print your articles in black ink (illegible articles will be returned). Must have original signatures.

NAME REQUIREMENTS:

The company name must include the words "Limited Liability Company" or the abbreviation "LLC" and may not include the words "Corporation" or "Incorporated."

For name availability, call 651-296-2803 between 8 a.m. and 4.30 p.m. (CT). A name may be reserved for a fee of $35.

ARTICLES SPECIAL REQUIREMENTS:

Registered agent is optional. SIC code should be provided from the following list of 19 choices:

00. Agriculture, Forestry, Fishing
10. Mining
15. Construction
20. Manufacturing–Non-Durable Goods
35. Manufacturing–Durable Goods
40. Transportation
48. Communications
49. Utilities
50. Wholesale trade
54. Retail - Non-Durable Goods
57. Retail - Durable Goods
60. Finance, Insurance, Real Estate
73. Business Services

80. Health Services
83. Social Services
86. Membership Organizations
87. Engineering and Management Services
89. Other Services
90. Other

If your LLC owns, leases or has interest in agricultural land as described in M.S. Section 500.24 this should be stated.

FILING FEES:

There is a filing fee of $135, payable to the "Secretary of State."

REPORTS:

Biennial report required.

RECORDS REQUIRED:

- Names and addresses of members and managers
- Articles and all amendments
- Three years of financial records
- Three years of tax returns
- Operating agreement and all amendments
- Voting rights
- Terms for distributions

STATUTES:

Chapter 322 B Minnesota Statutes.

MISSISSIPPI

Secretary of State
Business Services Division
P.O. Box 849
Jackson, MS 39205-0849
601-359-3593

Website: www.sos.state.ms.us/

State sends material within ten days.

WHAT THEY SUPPLY:

State provides computer-readable fill-in-the-blank forms with precise instructions how to meet the special requirements.

WHAT MUST BE FILED:

For computer legibility make sure you fill in the forms exactly as described in the instructions. File the original copy signed by the person forming the Limited Liability Company. Enclose the filing fee.

NAME REQUIREMENTS:

The company name must contain the words "Limited Liability Company," or the abbreviation "LLC" or "L.L.C." A name reservation is possible for a fee of $25.

ARTICLES SPECIAL REQUIREMENTS:

The Mississippi form is bar coded and meant to be machine-readable. Using their form will speed up your filing, but it is not required.

You need to provide the Federal Employer Identification Number (F.E.I.N.), which must be obtained prior to filing. This is obtained by filing IRS form SS-4 (form 3 in appendix C). If the number is needed quickly it can be obtained over the phone (404-455-2360), but you must have form SS-4 completed and in front of you.

The name of the company is limited to 120 characters on the bar-coded form, and some other information is limited in the number of characters allowed.

FILING FEES:

There is a filing fee of $50, payable to the "Secretary of State."

REPORTS:

No annual fee.

RECORDS REQUIRED:

- Names and addresses of members and managers
- Articles and all amendments
- Operating agreement and all amendments

STATUTES:

Mississippi Code beginning with Section 79-29-101.

MISSOURI

Corporations Division
600 W. Main, Room 322
Jefferson City, MO 65102-0778
573-751-1310 or 573-751-4153

Website: www.sos.state.mo.us

State sends material within one week.

WHAT THEY SUPPLY:

State provides two copies of fill-in-the-blank Articles of Organization. They provide few instructions in the form.

WHAT MUST BE FILED:

File the completed Articles in duplicate. Sign each copy and enclose the filing fee. If your documents conform to the filing provisions, the secretary will return the duplicate copy to the organizer.

NAME REQUIREMENTS:

The company name must contain the words "Limited Liability Company" or " Limited Company" or the abbreviation "L.L.C.," "L.C.," "LLC," or " LC." It may not contain the words "Corporation," "Incorporated," "Limited Partnership," or the abbreviation "Ltd." and must be distinguishable from any other corporate name already on file.

You can reserve a name for a fee of $25 by filing an application, which is available from the filing office.

ARTICLES SPECIAL REQUIREMENTS:

Missouri Statutes do not include any unusual requirements for the Articles.

FILING FEES:

There is a filing fee of $105, payable to the "Secretary of State."

REPORTS:

No annual fee.

RECORDS REQUIRED:

- Names and addresses of members and managers
- Articles and all amendments
- Three years of financial records
- Three years of tax returns
- Operating agreement and all amendments
- Voting rights
- Terms for distributions

STATUTES:

Chapter 347 Missouri Revised Statutes.

MONTANA

Secretary of State
P.O. Box 202801
Helena, MT 59620-2801
406-444-3665

Web site: www.sos.state.mt.us/css

State sends material within three weeks.

WHAT THEY SUPPLY:

State provides fill-in-the-blank Articles of Organization with guidelines how to complete them ("Help Sheet").

WHAT MUST BE FILED:

File the original and one copy of your signed Articles and enclose the correct filing fee.

"Priority filing" ensures twenty-four hour turn-around for an additional fee.

NAME REQUIREMENTS:

Your company name must contain the words or an abbreviation of "Limited Liability Company" or "Limited Company." If you want to perform professional service, the company name must contain the words (or abbreviation of) "Professional Limited Liability Company." A name reservation can be made for 120 days for a fee of $10. Fill out the application form provided by the state.

ARTICLES SPECIAL REQUIREMENTS:

The registered agent must sign the Articles. If there are managers, their names and residence addresses must be included; otherwise, the name and residence addresses of the members must be listed.

FILING FEES:

$70, payable to the "Secretary of State." Additional $20 for priority filing.

REPORTS:

Your annual report must be filed with the secretary of state prior to April 15 each year. The Secretary of State will mail the report to the corporation's regis-tered agent during January each year. The fee is $15, with an additional $15 due if it is filed after April 15th.

RECORDS REQUIRED:

- Names and addresses of members and managers
- Articles and all amendments
- Three years of financial records
- Three years of tax returns
- Operating agreement and all amendments

STATUTES:

Title 35, Chapter 8, Montana Code Annotated.

NEBRASKA

Secretary of State
Suite 1301 State Capitol
Lincoln, NE 68509
402-471-4079

Website: www.sos.state.ne.us

State sends material within three weeks.

WHAT THEY SUPPLY:

State provides fill-in-the-blank Articles of Organization in duplicate. No instructions are provided.

WHAT MUST BE FILED:

Two copies of the Articles.

NAME REQUIREMENTS:

The company name must contain the words "Limited Liability Company" or the abbreviation "L.L.C." You can reserve a name by filing the application provided by the state together with the appropriate fee of $15. If the name is available it will be reserved for 120 days.

ARTICLES SPECIAL REQUIREMENTS:

Must include the cash and property contributed as stated capital and events which will trigger the contribution of additional capital, if any. All managers' names and addresses, or if managed by members, all members' names and addresses must be listed.

Duration cannot exceed thirty years.

FILING FEES:

There is a filing fee of $110 plus $5 per page, made payable to the "Secretary of State."

REPORTS:

No annual filing fee.

RECORDS REQUIRED:

- Names and addresses of members and managers
- Articles and all amendments
- Three years of financial records
- Three years of tax returns
- Operating agreement and all amendments

STATUTES:

Chapter 21, beginning with Section 2601 Nebraska Limited Liability Company Act.

NEVADA

Secretary of State
Capitol Complex
Carson City, NV 89710
702-687-5203

Website: www.sos.state.nv.us/comm_rec
/index.htm

WHAT THEY SUPPLY:

State provides a comprehensive filing package with a list of registered agents, fill-in-the-blank Articles of Organization form, a copy of the Limited Liability Company Act, and a filing fee schedule.

WHAT MUST BE FILED:

File the original and as many copies of it as you want certified and returned to you. The articles must be acknowledged by a notary. Enclose the filing fee with an additional $20 for each certification.

NAME REQUIREMENTS:

The name must contain the words "Limited Liability Company," "Limited Company" or "Limited." You can abbreviate these terms as "L.L.C.," "LLC," or "LC." The name must be distinguishable from any other company name already on file in the filing office.

You can check for name availability by calling 775-684-5708. For a $20 fee, you can have a name reserved for ninety days.

ARTICLES SPECIAL REQUIREMENTS:

If the company is to be managed by managers, their names and addresses must be included, otherwise the names and addresses of the members must be included.

FILING FEE:

There is a filing fee of $175. The fee for a certified copy is $20 plus $1 per page.

REPORTS:

An annual report ("annual list") containing the main information about the company and its members must be filed with the secretary of state the month in which the anniversary date of its formation occurs. The report form is provided by the filing office. The annual fee is $85. If the report doesn't meet the requirements there will be an additional penalty of $50. The first list is due before the first day of the second month after the filing of its Articles of Organization. The initial list fee is $165.

The secretary of state will remind you of this report sixty days ahead of the last filing date.

RECORDS REQUIRED:

- Names and addresses of members and managers
- Articles and all amendments
- Three years of financial records
- Three years of tax returns
- Operating agreement and all amendments

STATUTES:

Chapter 86 Nevada Revised Statutes.

NEW HAMPSHIRE

Secretary of State
107 N. Main Street
Concord, NH 03301-4989
603-271-3244

Website: www.state.nh.us/sos

State sends material within one week.

WHAT THEY SUPPLY:

State provides two copies of the fill-in-the-blank form of Certificate of Formation with instructions. It also provides one copy of the form Addendum to Certificate of Formation.

WHAT MUST BE FILED:

The Certificate of Formation must be filed in duplicate and signed by a member or manager with his or her capacity designated. It must be accompanied by form LCC 1-A, Addendum to Certificate of Formation.

NAME REQUIREMENTS:

Your company name must contain the words "Limited Liability Company," the abbreviation "L.L.C.," or a similar abbreviation.

The name may contain the words "Company," "Association," "Club," "Foundation," "Fund," "Institute," "Society," "Union," "Syndicate," "Trust," "Limited," or abbreviations of these words.

If the company will perform professional services, the company name must end with the words "Professional Limited Liability Company" or the abbreviation "P.L.L.C."

It must be distinguishable from any other company name already on file.

A name reservation for a period of 120 days can be obtained by the filing office.

ARTICLES SPECIAL REQUIREMENTS:

The Certificate of Formation must list the nature of the primary business, but you may add the authority "to perform any lawful business permitted for limited liability companies under the state law." In New Hampshire, your LLC must certify in a separate Addendum (Form LLC 1-A) that it meets the requirements of the New Hampshire Securities Law. If the aggregate number of holders of the company's securities does not exceed ten, provides that no advertising has been published in connection with any security sale, and all securities sales are consummated within sixty days after the date of the formation of the company, then the company is exempt from securities registration. If your company meets these requirements, check line 1. in the Addendum. If your company has or will register its securities for sale in New Hampshire, enter the date the registration statement was or will be filed with the Bureau of Securities Regulation in line 2. If you can take advantage of another exemption from the registration requirement, cite this exemption in line 3.

FILING FEES:

The filing fee for the Certificate of Formation is $35 and for the Addendum, $50–a total of $85.

REPORTS:

A first annual report must be delivered to the secretary of state between January 1 and April 1 of the year following the calendar year in which the LLC was formed. The annual fee is $100 and there is a $50 additional fee if it is late. The annual report forms are sent to you by the state in January.

RECORDS REQUIRED:

- Names and addresses of members and managers
- Articles and all amendments
- Three years of financial records
- Three years of tax returns
- Operating agreement and all amendments

STATUTES:

New Hampshire Revised Statutes Annotated, beginning with Section 304-C:1.

New Jersey

Secretary of State
Division of Commercial Recording
P. O. Box 300
Trenton, NJ 08625
609-530-6400

Website: www.state.nj.us/njbiz

WHAT THEY SUPPLY:

State provides fill-in-the-blank Certificate of Formation form, as well as a fax filing program with instructions and a Fax Filing Service Request form for faster filing procedure.

WHAT MUST BE FILED:

You need to file the "Public Records Filing for New Business Entity" form and the "Business Registration" form. Those forms are for any new business, so make sure to check that you are forming a limited liability company.

To take part in the fax-filing program which offers same or next day filing, complete the "Facsimile Filing Service Request" and fax this request together with your completed Certificate of Formation to 609-984-6851. Payment method for this program is either by Visa/MC or Discover, or you have to give your depository account number. Note that there is an extra filing fee for the fax service (see "Filing Fees" below).

NAME REQUIREMENTS:

The company name must contain the words "Limited Liability Company" or the abbreviation "L.L.C."

There is a $50 name reservation fee. For more information on name availability reservation, call 609-292-9292.

ARTICLES SPECIAL REQUIREMENTS:

You need to put in a type code in No. 2. The type code for your limited liability company is "LLC" (for a foreign: "FLC").

FILING FEES:

The regular filing fee is $125. If you want expedited service (requests must be delivered in person or by messenger service), add an additional $10 fee.

For the fax filing service, there's also a $10 fee for expedited service (next business day filing) or $50 fee for same-day filing. Note that there's a $1 per page fee for all filings that are faxed back.

REPORTS:

No annual filing fee.

RECORDS REQUIRED:

- Operating agreement and all amendments
- Minutes of meetings

STATUTES:

New Jersey Revised Statutes Title 42:2B.

NEW MEXICO

Public Regulation Commission
1120 Paseo de Peralta
PERA Bldg., Room 536
P.O. Box 1269
Santa Fe, NM 87504-1269
505-827-4500

Website: www.nmprc.state.nm.us/corporation.htm

State sends material within two weeks.

WHAT THEY SUPPLY:

State provides complete filing package for domestic and foreign LLCs. This includes fill-in-the-blank forms with instructions.

WHAT MUST BE FILED:

An original and duplicate of Articles of Organization together with the notarized affidavit of the person appointed as your registered agent. Enclose the appropriate filing fee.

The filing office also accepts faxed filing documents.

NAME REQUIREMENTS:

The company name must contain the words "Limited Liability Company" or "Limited Company", or the abbreviation "L.L.C.," "LLC," "L.C." or "LC." The word "Limited" may be abbreviated as "Ltd." and the word "Company" as "Co."

Use the Application form to reserve your desired name for a 120 day reservation for a fee of $20.

ARTICLES SPECIAL REQUIREMENTS:

A notarized affidavit accepting appointment must be provided by the registered agent.

FILING FEES:

There is a $50 fee for filing the Articles. If you want a certification there's another $25 for this service. The fees must be paid to the "State Corporation Commission."

REPORTS:

No annual fee.

RECORDS REQUIRED:

- No requirement

STATUTES:

New Mexico Statutes Annotated Title 53, Chapter 19.

NEW YORK

NYS Department of State
Division of Corporations
41 State Street
Albany, N.Y. 12231
518-473-2492 or
518-474-6200

Website: www.dos.state.ny.us/corp/corpwww.html

State sends material within one week.

WHAT THEY SUPPLY:

State provides one copy of fill-in-the-blank Articles of Organization, one form to apply for a name reservation, a fee schedule, and a booklet, "Forming a Limited Liability Company in New York State," with instructions.

WHAT MUST BE FILED:

An original and duplicate of Articles of Organization.

If you reserved a name prior to filing, enclose a copy of the certificate of name registration.

NAME REQUIREMENTS:

Your company name must contain the words "Limited Liability Company" or the abbreviation "L.L.C." or "LLC." It must be distinguishable from any other existing LLC name. It may not contain words or phrases related to banks, insurance businesses, trusts or finance business without prior approval. See Section 204 of the New York LLC law for details.

You can reserve a name for 60 days for a fee of $20 using the application form provided by the state.

ARTICLES SPECIAL REQUIREMENTS:

The secretary of state should be designated as agent for service of process. The county of the principal office must be listed.

Notice of formation must be published in two publications of general circulation, once a week for six weeks.

FILING FEES:

There is a $200 fee for filing the Articles of Organization, payable to the "Department of State."

REPORTS:

In New York, you have to submit a report every two years in the calendar month during which the Articles of Organization were filed. The fee for this biennial report is only $9.

RECORDS REQUIRED:

- Names and addresses of members and managers
- Articles and all amendments
- Three years of financial records
- Three years of tax returns
- Operating agreement and all amendments
- Members' contributions
- Members allocations and distributions

STATUTES:

Chapter 34 of the Consolidated Law, New York Limited Liability Company Law.

NORTH CAROLINA

Corporations Division
P.O. Box 29622
Raleigh, NC 27626-0622
919-807-2225

Website: www.secretary.state.nc.us./corporations

State sends material within ten days.

WHAT THEY SUPPLY:

State provides booklet, "Organizing Your Limited Liability Company in North Carolina," with fill-in-the-blank froms and detailed instructions.

WHAT MUST BE FILED:

An original and duplicate of Articles of Organization.

NAME REQUIREMENTS:

The company name must contain the words "Limited Liability Company," "L.L.C.," "Ltd. Liability Co.," "Limited Liability Co.," "LLC," or "Ltd. Liability Company."

A name can be reserved for a fee of $10.

ARTICLES SPECIAL REQUIREMENTS:

Name and address of each organizer is required.

FILING FEES:

There is a filing fee of $125, payable to the "Secretary of State." Same day service is available for $200 additional or twenty-four hour service for an additional $100.

REPORTS:

Annual report with $200 fee. It is due by the fifteenth day of the fourth month following the close of the LLC's fiscal year.

RECORDS REQUIRED:

- Names and addresses of members and managers
- Articles and all amendments
- Five years of financial records
- Five years of tax returns
- Operating agreement and all amendments

STATUTES:

North Carolina General Statutes Title 57C.

North Dakota

Secretary of State
600 East Boulevard Avenue, Dept. 108
Bismarck, ND 58505-0500
701-328-4284 or 800-352-0687 ext. 4284

Website: www.state.nd.us/sec

State sends material within two weeks.

WHAT THEY SUPPLY:

Filing office provides a booklet about how to form your LLC and how to draft your Articles of Organization. Included is a sample of completed articles and a "Registered Agent Consent to Serve" form. They also send you a copy of the Limited Liability Company Act at no charge.

WHAT MUST BE FILED:

An original and duplicate of Articles of Organization and a Registered Agent Consent to Serve.

NAME REQUIREMENTS:

The company name must contain the words "Limited Liability Company" or the abbreviation "L.L.C." or "LLC." It may not contain words as "Bank," "Banker," or "Banking" and must be distinguishable from any other company name existing.

A company name may be reserved for $10.

ARTICLES SPECIAL REQUIREMENTS:

Must include name and address of each organizer.

FILING FEES:

There is a $125 fee for filing the Articles of Organization plus an additional $10 for filing the consent of the registered agent for a total of $135.

REPORTS:

Your LLC must file an annual report by November 15 each year. The secretary of state will mail annual report forms to the registered agent. The filing fee for the annual report is $50.

RECORDS REQUIRED:

- Names and addresses of members
- Articles and all amendments
- Five years of financial records
- Five years of tax returns
- Minutes of meetings
- Members' contributions

STATUTES:

North Dakota Century Code. Chapter 10-32.

OHIO

Secretary of State
Corporations Division
180 E. Broad Street, 16th Floor
Columbus, OH 43215
614-466-3910

Website: www.state.oh.us/sos

State sends material within ten days.

WHAT THEY SUPPLY:

State provides fill-in-the-blank form of Articles of Organization with instructions and an "Original Appointment of Agent" form which has to be signed by the registered agent.

WHAT MUST BE FILED:

One copy of each of Articles of Organization and Original Appointment of Agent. The Appointment must be signed by a majority of members and by the agent.

NAME REQUIREMENTS:

Your company name must contain the words "Limited Liability Company," "Limited," or the abbreviation "L.L.C." or "Ltd."

For name availability, call the filing office. A name reservation can be made for a $5 fee for sixty days.

ARTICLES SPECIAL REQUIREMENTS:

The Articles must be accompanied by an Original Appointment of Agent signed by a majority of members and by the agent.

FILING FEE:

There is a filing fee of $125, payable to the "Ohio Secretary of State."

REPORTS:

No annual report.

RECORDS REQUIRED:

- Names and addresses of members and managers
- Articles and all amendments
- Three years of financial records
- Three years of tax returns
- Operating agreement and all amendments
- Voting rights

STATUTES:

Title 17, Chapter 1705 of the Ohio Revised Code, Limited Liability Companies.

OKLAHOMA

Secretary of State, Business Filing Department
2300 N. Lincoln Boulevard, Room 101
101 State Capitol Building
Oklahoma City, OK 73105-4897
405-521-3912

Website: www.sos.state.ok.us

State sends material within ten days.

WHAT THEY SUPPLY:

State provides fill-in-the-blank forms of Articles of Organization in duplicate together with filing instructions.

WHAT MUST BE FILED:

Two copies of the Articles must be filed.

NAME REQUIREMENTS:

Your company name must contain the words "Limited Liability Company" or "Limited Company," or the abbreviation "L.L.C.," "LLC," "LC,"or "L.C." The word "Limited" may be abbreviated as "Ltd." and the word "Company" as "Co." The name must be distinguishable from any other corporation name existing or having existed during the preceding three years.

Name availability may be checked by calling the secretary of state at 405-522-4560. A name may be reserved for a period of sixty days by filing a name reservation application and a fee of $10.

ARTICLES SPECIAL REQUIREMENTS:

No unusual requirements.

FILING FEES:

There is a filing fee of $100, payable to the "Oklahoma Secretary of State."

REPORTS:

No annual report.

RECORDS REQUIRED:

- Names and addresses of members and managers
- Articles and all amendments
- Three years of financial records
- Three years of tax returns
- Past members and managers

STATUTES:

Title 18, Chapter 32 of the Oklahoma Statutes, Oklahoma Limited Liability Company Act.

OREGON

State of Oregon
Corporation Division
255 Capitol Street NE, Suite 151
Salem, OR 97310-1327
503-986-2200
Fax: 503-378-4381

Website: www.filinginoregon.com

WHAT THEY SUPPLY:

State provides complete business package including the "Oregon Business Guide," which gives detailed information on all kinds of businesses. The package also includes tax tables, an Employers' Registration form, an application for the Employer Identification Number (IRS form SS-4) and a fill-in-the-blank Articles of Organization form.

WHAT MUST BE FILED:

Original and one copy.

NAME REQUIREMENTS:

The name must contain the words "Limited Liability Company" or the abbreviation "L.L.C." or "LLC." It must be distinguishable from any other company name already on file.

For name availability call (503) 986-2200. For a name reservation send an application and a $10 fee to the filing office. If the name is available, it will be reserved for 120 days.

ARTICLES SPECIAL REQUIREMENTS:

Name and address of each organizer must be included.

FILING FEES:

There is a fee of $20 for filing the Articles, payable to the "Corporation Division." Fees can be paid by check, Visa, or MasterCard.

REPORTS:

The annual report must be delivered to the secretary of state on the anniversary date of your LLC. The annual report form is sent to the registered agent forty-five days prior to the due date. The annual fee is $30.

RECORDS REQUIRED:

- Names and addresses of members and managers
- Principle business address
- Registered agent name and address
- Federal employer identification number

STATUTES:

Title 7, Chapter 63 Oregon Revised Statutes, Oregon Limited Liability Company Act.

PENNSYLVANIA

Department of State
Corporation Bureau
P.O. Box 8722
Harrisburg, PA 17105-8722
717-787-1057

Website: www.state.pa.us

State sends material within three weeks.

WHAT THEY SUPPLY:

State provides fill-in-the-blank forms of Certificate of Organization with instructions. They also include the docketing statement, which must be filed with your certificate.

WHAT MUST BE FILED:

One original Certificate of Organization–Domestic Limited Liability Company and one copy of the completed docketing statement (form DSCB:15-134A).

Also include either a self-addressed, stamped postcard with the filing information noted or a self-addressed, stamped envelope with a copy of the filing document to receive confirmation of the file date prior to receiving the microfilmed original.

NAME REQUIREMENTS:

The company name must contain the words "Limited," "Company," or "Limited Liability Company," or abbreviations of these words.

Name availability can be checked either by a written request or by phone at 717-787-1057. The fee for an availability of three names is $12.

A name reservation can only be made by a written request together with a $52 fee. The reservation is good for 120 days. You will get a confirmation of your reservation by mail.

ARTICLES SPECIAL REQUIREMENTS:

Must list names and addresses of all members and organizers.

FILING FEE:

There is a $100 fee, payable to the "Department of State."

REPORTS:

There's an annual registration fee of at least $360, also payable to the "Department of State." The report must be filed every year before April 15.

RECORDS REQUIRED:

- Names and addresses of members and managers
- Articles and all amendments
- Operating agreement and all amendments

STATUTES:

Title 15, Chapter 89, Pennsylvania Consolidated Statutes.

RHODE ISLAND

Secretary of State
100 N. Main Street
Providence, RI 02903
401-222-3040

Website:
www.state.ri.us/corporations.htm

State sends material within one week.

WHAT THEY SUPPLY:

State provides fill-in-the-blank Articles of Organization in duplicate. Instructions are also provided.

WHAT MUST BE FILED:

Two signed copies of the Articles of Organization must be filed.

NAME REQUIREMENTS:

The name must end with the words "Limited Liability Company" or the abbreviation "L.L.C." or "LLC," either in upper or lower case letters. The name may not be similar to the name of any entity on file with the Corporations Division.

For name availability call the filing office at 401-222-3040, a name reservation can be made for a fee of $50.

ARTICLES SPECIAL REQUIREMENTS:

A statement should be included indicating whether the company is to be taxed as a corporation or pass-through entity.

FILING FEES:

There is a filing fee of $150, payable to the "Secretary of State.

REPORTS:

An annual report must be filed each calendar year between September 1 and November 1, beginning the year after the original Articles of Organization are filed. The Report form will be mailed to the resident agent prior to September 1 each year. The annual fee is $50.

RECORDS REQUIRED:

- Names and addresses of members and managers
- Articles and all amendments
- Five years of financial records
- Five years of tax returns
- Operating agreement and all amendments

STATUTES:

Title 7, Chapter 16 of the General Laws of Rhode Island.

SOUTH CAROLINA

Secretary of State
P.O. Box 11350
Columbia, SC 29211
803-734-2158

Website: www.scsos.com

WHAT THEY SUPPLY:

State provides fill-in-the-blank Articles of Organization with instructions. For $2, they will send an IBM format computer diskette containing the forms.

WHAT MUST BE FILED:

File the completed original and one copy (duplicate, original, or conformed copy). Enclose the filing fee.

NAME REQUIREMENTS:

Your company name must contain the words "Limited Liability Company," "Limited Company" or the abbreviation "L.L.C.," "LLC," "L.C.," or "LC." The words "Limited" and " Company" may be abbreviated as "Ltd." and "Co."

A name can be reserved for 120 days for a fee of $25.

ARTICLES SPECIAL REQUIREMENTS:

On the Articles of Organization form provided by the state, article 7 allows the company to designate one or more of its members to be liable for company debts. This is neither required nor recommended and defeats the purpose of the limited liability company.

FILING FEES:

There is a filing fee of $110, payable to the "Secretary of State."

REPORTS:

The initial report is due between January 1 and April 1 of the year following the calendar year in which the limited liability company was organized. Subsequent reports must be delivered to the secretary of state before the fifteenth day of the fourth month following the close of the taxable year of the limited liability company. The fee is $10.

RECORDS REQUIRED:

- Names and addresses of members and managers
- Articles and all amendments
- Six years of financial records
- Six years of tax returns
- Operating agreement and all amendments

STATUTES:

Chapter 33-44 of the South Carolina Code of 1976.

SOUTH DAKOTA

Secretary of State
State Capital
500 E. Capital Street
Pierre, SD 57501
605-773-4845

Website: www.state.sd.us/sos/sos.htm

State sends material within one week.

WHAT THEY SUPPLY:

State provides fill-in-the-blank form of Articles of Organization and the first Annual Report.

WHAT MUST BE FILED:

Two copies of the Articles of Organization and a First Annual Report.

NAME REQUIREMENTS:

Your company name must contain the words "Limited Liability Company", "Limited Company" or the abbreviation "L.L.C.," "LLC," "L.C.," or "LC." It must be distinguishable from any corporation name on file.

A name reservation can be made by filing an application with the secretary of state. If the name is available, it will be reserved for 120 days.

ARTICLES SPECIAL REQUIREMENTS:

The duration of the LLC can be for no more than thirty years (though it can be extended in the future). Total cash, property and services contributed must be listed as well as requirements for future contributions.

If there are managers, their names and residence addresses must be included; otherwise, the name and residence addresses of the members must be listed.

On the Articles of Organization form provided by the state, article 7 allows the company to designate one or more of its members to be liable for company debts. This is neither required nor recommended and defeats the purpose of the limited liability company.

A first Annual Report must be filed along with the Articles.

FILING FEES:

For companies with capital of up to $50,000, the fee is $90; for $50,001 to $100,000 it is $150. Above $100,000, it is an additional $0.50 per $1,000 with a maximum fee of $16,000.

REPORTS:

After the first Annual Report the filing fee for subsequent reports is $50 unless the report reflects an increase in capital. In such case the fees above must be paid.

RECORDS REQUIRED:

- Names and addresses of members and managers
- Articles and all amendments
- Three years of financial records
- Three years of tax returns
- Operating agreement and all amendments

STATUTES:

South Dakota Codified Laws, Title 47, Chapters 34 and 34A.

TENNESSEE

Department of State
Corporate Filings
312 Eighth Avenue North
6th Floor, William R. Snodgrass Tower
Nashville, TN 37243
615-741-2286

Website: www.state.tn.us/sos/service.htm

State sends material within one week.

WHAT THEY SUPPLY:

State provides a comprehensive and detailed "Filing Guide" for Limited Liability Companies, which contains all the forms you need and a fee schedule.

WHAT MUST BE FILED:

Only one original Articles of Organization must be filed.

NAME REQUIREMENTS:

The name must contain the words "limited liability company" or the abbreviation "L.L.C." or "LLC." It may not contain the words "Corporation" or "Incorporated" and must be distinguishable from any other name on file with the filing office.

If you want to perform professional service, your company name must contain the words "Professional Limited Company", "Professional Limited Liability Company," "Limited Liability Professional Company," "Professional LLC" or the abbreviation "P.L.C.," "P.L.L.C.," "PLC," "PLLC" or "L.L.P.C."

For name availability, call 615-741-2286. A name reservation can be made by filing an application with the Division of Business Service together with a $20 fee.

ARTICLES SPECIAL REQUIREMENTS:

The name and address of each organizer must be listed. The county and zip code of the registered office and the principle executive office must be included with their addresses. The number of members must be listed.

If a member can be expelled and if there are prescriptive rights, these must be spelled out in the Articles. It is possible to designate one or more of its members to be liable for company debts. This is neither required nor recommended, as it defeats the purpose of the limited liability company.

FILING FEES:

The filing fee is $50 per member on the date of filing with a minimum of $300 and a maximum of $3000. The fee can be paid either by check, bank draft or money order, payable to the "Tennessee Secretary of State." There is also a $20 county recording fee.

REPORTS:

The annual report must be filed on or before the first day of the fourth month following the close of the LLC's fiscal year. The report form will be sent to the registered office one month prior to the end of the LLC's fiscal year. The fee for the annual report is–like the fee for filing the articles–$50 per member on the date of filing, with a minimum of $300 and a maximum of $3000. There is an additional $20 due if the registered agent changes.

RECORDS REQUIRED:

- Names and addresses of members and managers
- Articles and all amendments
- Three years of financial records
- Three years of tax returns
- Operating agreement and all amendments
- Minutes of all proceedings
- Last annual report
- Any assignments

STATUTES:

Tennessee Code Annotated, Sections 48-201-101 through 48-248-606.

TEXAS

Corporations Section
Statutory Filings Division
Office of the Secretary of State
P.O. Box 13697
Austin, TX 78711-3697
512-463-5555

Website: www.sos.state.tx.us/corp/index.shtml

State sends material within two weeks.

WHAT THEY SUPPLY:

State provdies one copy of fill-in-the-blank Articles of Organization with instructions. You can get additional forms by visiting the website or by calling 900-263-0060.

WHAT MUST BE FILED:

Two copies of the Articles must be filed. Use the P. O. box for mail. For courier use: James Earl Rudder Office Building, 1019 Brazos, Austin, TX 78701.

NAME REQUIREMENTS:

The name must contain the words "Limited Liability Company" or "Limited Company," or the abbreviations "L.L.C.," "LLC," "LC," "L.C.," or "Ltd.Co." It may not be the same or similar to that of any other LLC, corporation or partnership on file. For name availability call 512-463-5555, or email corpinfo@sos.state.tx.us prior to filing. A name reservation can be made for a fee of $25 for a period of 120 days.

ARTICLES SPECIAL REQUIREMENTS:

The name and address of each organizer must be included.

FILING FEES:

There is a filing fee of $200, payable to the "Secretary of State."

REPORTS:

Annual report fee is based upon the amount of capital and earned surplus in the company.

RECORDS REQUIRED:

- Names and addresses of members and managers
- Articles and all amendments
- Six years of financial records
- Six years of tax returns
- Contributions

STATUTES:

Texas Rev. Civil Statutes Annotated art. 1528n, Texas Limited Liability Company Act.

UTAH

Department of Commerce
Division of Corporations and Commercial Code
S.M. Box 146705
Salt Lake City, UT 84114-6705
801-530-4849

Website: www.utah.gov/business/generalinfo.html

State sends material within one week.

WHAT THEY SUPPLY:

State provides guidelines how to draft your own Articles of Organization. It also provides information on organizing a professional LLC.

WHAT MUST BE FILED:

File one original and one exact copy of your Articles. You can deliver the documents personally, by mail or by fax. If you choose to fax your documents, make sure to include the number of your Visa/MasterCard and the expiration date.

NAME REQUIREMENTS:

Your company name must include the words "Limited Liability Company," "Limited Company," or the abbreviation "L.C." or "L.L.C."

ARTICLES SPECIAL REQUIREMENTS:

The period of duration cannot exceed ninety-nine years. If there are managers, their names and residence addresses must be included, otherwise the name and residence addresses of the members must be listed.

FILING FEES:

There is a filing fee of $50, payable to the "Division of Corporations and Commercial Code."

REPORTS:

The annual report must be filed in the month of the anniversary date the company was created. The Division of Corporations sends an annual report notice and a reporting form to the registered agent prior to the filing date. The fee is $10.

RECORDS REQUIRED:

- Names and addresses of members and managers
- Articles and all amendments
- Three years of financial records
- Three years of tax returns
- Operating agreement and all amendments
- Contributions

STATUTES:

Utah Code Annotated, Title 48-2B.

VERMONT

Secretary of State
81 River Street, Drawer 09
Montpelier, VT 05609
802-828-2386

Website: www.sec.state.vt.us/corps/corpindex.htm

State sends materials within one week.

WHAT THEY SUPPLY:

State provides fill-in-the-blank form of Articles of Organization with basic instructions.

WHAT MUST BE FILED:

The original and one exact copy.

NAME REQUIREMENTS:

Your company name must contain the words "Limited Liability Company," "Limited Company" or the abbreviation "LLC" or "LC." The words "Limited" and "Company" may be abbreviated "Ltd." and "Co."

A name can be reserved for 120 days for a fee of $20.

ARTICLES SPECIAL REQUIREMENTS:

The name and address of each organizer are required.

It is possible to designate one or more of the company's members to be liable for company debts. This is neither required nor recommended, as it defeats the purpose of the limited liability company. However, you need to include a statement about it in your articles.

FILING FEES:

There is a filing fee of $75, payable to the "Vermont Secretary of State."

REPORTS:

An annual report must be filed within two and a half months after the end of your fiscal year. The report form will be mailed to your registered agent in advance. The fee is $15.

RECORDS REQUIRED:

- Names and addresses of members and managers
- Articles and all amendments
- Three years of financial records
- Three years of tax returns
- Three years operating agreements

STATUTES:

Vermont Statutes Annotated, Title 11, Chapter 21, beginning with Section 3001.

VIRGINIA

Clerk of the State Corporation Commission
P.O. Box 1197
Richmond, VA 23218-1197
804-371-9733

Website: www.state.va.us/scc/division/clk

State sends material within two weeks.

WHAT THEY SUPPLY:

State provides fill-in-the-blank Articles of Organization with simple instructions and a fee schedule.

WHAT MUST BE FILED:

The Articles must be printed or typewritten in black ink. Complete and file the original form and enclose the filing fee.

NAME REQUIREMENTS:

The name must contain the words "Limited Company" or "Limited Liability Company" or the abbreviations "L.C.," "LC," "L.L.C.," or "LLC."

A name reservation can be made for 120 days by filing an application (form LLC-1013) with a $10 fee.

ARTICLES SPECIAL REQUIREMENTS:

The registered agent must be an individual who is a Virginia resident and either a member or an officer, director or partner of a member of the LLC, or a Virginia State Bar member, or an organization registered under Va. Code Section 54.1-3902 (an attorney's PC, PLLC, or PRLLP) and this must be stated in the Articles.

The city or county of the registered agent must be included and also the post office address of the office where the records will be kept.

The Articles can be executed by any person.

FILING FEES:

There is a filing fee of $100, payable to the "State Corporation Commission." Pay by check or similar payment method, no cash accepted. A certified copy is $6.

REPORTS:

Annual report required with $50 filing fee. The fee is due each year before September 1, beginning the year after the calendar year in which your company was organized.

RECORDS REQUIRED:

- Names and addresses of members and managers
- Articles and all amendments
- Three years of financial records
- Three years of tax returns
- Three years operating agreements

STATUTES:

Title 13.1 of the Code of Virginia.

WASHINGTON

Secretary of State
Corporations Division
P.O. Box 40234
Olympia, WA 98504-0234
360-753-7115

Website: www.secstate.wa.gov

State sends material within one week.

WHAT THEY SUPPLY:

State provides single copy of fill-in-the-blank Certificate of Formation form.

WHAT MUST BE FILED:

Type or print the document in black ink. Submit original and one copy. If expedited service is desired write "expedited" in bold letters on outside of envelope and include the additional fee.

NAME REQUIREMENTS:

Your company name must contain the words "Limited Liability Company," "Limited Liability Co." or the abbreviation "L.L.C." or "LLC."

For a $30 fee, you can reserve an LLC name for a period of 180 days.

ARTICLES SPECIAL REQUIREMENTS:

There are no unusual requirements.

FILING FEES:

There is a filing fee of $175, payable to the "Secretary of State". Expedited service of twenty-four hour turn around is available for an additional $20.

REPORTS:

Your first annual report has to be filed within 120 days of filing your Certificate of Formation. The fee is $10. After that your annual report is due on the date determined by the secretary of state. The report form is provided by the secretary of state.

RECORDS REQUIRED:

- Names and addresses of members and managers
- Articles and all amendments
- Three years of financial records
- Three years of tax returns
- Operating agreement and amendments
- Past members and managers
- Contributions

STATUTES:

Chapter 25.15 Revised Code of Washington.

WEST VIRGINIA

Secretary of State
Building 1, Suite 157-K
1900 Kanawha Boulevard East
Charleston, WV 25305-0770
304-558-8000

Website: www.state.wv.us/sos/

State sends materials within one week.

WHAT THEY SUPPLY:

State provides a booklet, "Applications and Instructions for Business Start-Up," instructions for filing Articles of Organization, and two copies of fill-in-the-blank Articles of Organization.

WHAT MUST BE FILED:

Two original copies of the Articles of Organization must be filed.

NAME REQUIREMENTS:

Your company name must contain the words "Limited Liability Company," "Limited Company," or the abbreviations "LLC," L.L.C.," "LC," or "L.C." "Limited" and "company" may not be abbreviated as "Ltd." and "Co." It may not use the words "Corporation," "Incorporated," "Limited Partnership," or the abbreviations "Corp.," or "Inc."

Professional companies must use "Professional Limited Liability Company," "Professional L.L.C.," "Professional LLC," "P.L.L.C.," or "PLLC."

Name may be reserved for 120 days for $15.

ARTICLES SPECIAL REQUIREMENTS:

It is possible to designate members to be liable for company debts. This is neither required nor recommended, as it defeats the purpose of the limited liability company. However, the statement needs to be included in your articles.

FILING FEES:

There is a filing fee of $100, payable to the "Secretary of State." Add $15 for each certified copy of Articles requested.

REPORTS:

The annual report is due each year between January 1 and April 1. The fee is $25.

RECORDS REQUIRED:

- No requirement

STATUTES:

Chapter 31B, beginning with Section 1-101, Uniform Limited Liability Company Act.

WISCONSIN

Department of Financial Institutions
Division of Corporate and Consumer Services
P.O. Box 7846
Madison, WI 53707-7846
608-261-7577

Website: www.wisconsin.gov
or www.wdfi.org/corporations

State sends material within one week.

WHAT THEY SUPPLY:

State provides two copies of fill-in-the-blank Articles of Organization with instruction sheet and fee schedule.

WHAT MUST BE FILED:

Original and one copy must be filed.

For expedited service (filing procedure will be complete the next business day), mark your documents "For Expedited Service" and provide an extra $25 for each item. Indicate on the back side of your Articles where you would like the acknowledgement copy of the filed document sent.

Use the above address for mail. For courier delivery use 345 W. Washington Ave., 3rd Fl., Madison, WI 53703.

NAME REQUIREMENTS:

Your company name must contain the words "Limited Liability Company" or "Limited Liability Co." or must end with the abbreviations "L.L.C." or "LLC."

For name availability, call the filing office prior to filing. A name can be reserved either by calling 608-261-9555 or by a written application. The application must include the name and address of the applicant and the name proposed to be reserved. If the name is available, it will be reserved for 120 days. The reservation fee is $15 by mail or $30 by phone. The name can be renewed for an additional 120 days for the same fees.

If your first choice is not available, you can provide a second choice name on the reverse side of your Articles.

ARTICLES REQUIREMENT:

The Articles for a Wisconsin LLC can *only* contain items of information:

- The name
- The street address of the initial registered office
- The name of the initial registered agent at the above address
- Whether management is vested in the members or manager(s)
- The name, address and signature of each organizer
- A statement that the company is organized under Wisconsin statutes, chapter 183
- The name of the person who drafted the articles

Other terms between members can be included in the operating agreement.

FILING FEES:

There is a $170 filing fee. For expedited service, add an additional $25 for each item. If you file your Articles electronically via the Internet (www.wdfi.org, click on "Quickstart LLC"), the filing fee is $130, including the charge for expedited processing. If you file via Internet the fee is only payable by Visa or Mastercard.

REPORTS:

No annual reporting fee.

RECORDS REQUIRED:

- Names and addresses of members and managers
- Articles and all amendments
- Three years of financial records
- Three years of tax returns
- Operating agreement and amendments
- Must be kept in principal office

STATUTES:

Chapter 183 of the Wisconsin Statutes.

WYOMING

Secretary of State
State Capitol Building
Cheyenne, WY 82002-0020
307-777-7311

Website: http://soswy.state.wy.us/corporat
/corporat.htm

State sends material within two weeks.

WHAT THEY SUPPLY:

State provides fill-in-the-blank form of Articles of Organization and "Consent to Appointment by Registered Agent" with instructions how to complete these forms.

WHAT MUST BE FILED:

An original and one exact copy must be filed along with a written consent to appointment by the registered agent.

NAME REQUIREMENTS:

The company name must contain the words "Limited Liability Company" or "Limited Company," or the abbreviation "L.L.C.," "LLC," "L.C.," or "LC." It can also contain the combination "Ltd Liability Co." or "Limited Liability Co." or "Ltd. Liability Company."

A name can be reserved for a fee of $50 for a 120 day period.

ARTICLES SPECIAL REQUIREMENTS:

The total of cash, a description, the agreed value of property other than cash contributed to the company, and any additional capital agreed to be contributed must be included in the Articles.

If there is a right to admit new members the terms of admission must be stated.

If the members have a right to continue the business after the termination of a member this must be stated.

The Articles must accompany a written consent by the registered agent to appointment as agent.

FILING FEES:

The filing fee is $100.

REPORTS:

The annual report is due on the first day of the month of registration. The fee is $50 or two tenths of one million on the dollar ($.0002), whichever is greater based on the company's assets located and employed in the state of Wyoming.

RECORDS REQUIRED:

- Written operating agreement
- Minutes of meetings

STATUTES:

Wyoming Statute beginning with 17-15-101.

APPENDIX B
SAMPLE FILLED-IN FORMS

Transmittal Letter

To: Secretary of State
      Corporation Division
      State Capitol, Rm 100
      Libertyville, FL 33757

Re: Williams and Johnson, L.L.C.

Enclosed is an original and ____1____ copies of articles of organization for the above-referenced LLC along with a check for $125_____ as follows:

        $__125___ for filing fee
        $__---___ for _____

Please send acknowledgement of receipt and/or date-stamped copy to:

      Bill Williams
      Williams and Johnson, L.L.C.
      123 Liberty Street
      Libertyville, FL 33757

ARTICLES OF ORGANIZATION FOR A LIMITED LIABILITY COMPANY

ARTICLE I - Name:

The name of the Limited Liability Company is:

Williams and Johnson, L.L.C.

ARTICLE II - Purpose:

The purpose for which this limited liability company is organized is:

to engage in any and all lawful acts for which an L.L.C. may be formed.

ARTICLE III - Duration:

The period of duration for the Limited Liability Company shall be: perpetual

ARTICLE IV - Registered (or Statutory) Agent and Address:

The name and address of the initial registered (statutory) agent is:

Bill Williams, 123 Liberty Street, Libertyville, FL 33757

ARTICLE V - Management:
(Check the appropriate box and complete the statement)

☐ The Limited Liability Company is to be managed by a manager or managers and the name(s) and address(es) of such manager(s) who is/are to serve as manager(s) is/are:

☒ The Limited Liability Company is to be managed by the members and the name(s) and address(es) of the managing members is/are:

Bill Williams, 123 Liberty Street, Libertyville, FL 33757

John Johnson, 605 Leisure Lane, Libertyville, FL 33756

ARTICLE VI - Principal Place of Business

The initial principal place of business of the limited liability company is:

123 Liberty Street, Libertyville, FL 33757

ARTICLE VII - Effective Date

The effective date of these articles is ☒ upon filing   ☐ on _____

ARTICLE VIII - Nonliability

The members and managers, if any, shall not be liable for any debts, obligations or liabilities of the limited liability company.

ARTICLE IX - Miscellaneous

New members can be admitted to the company with full rights of membership upon the unanimous consent of the existing members.

IN WITNESS WHEREOF, the undersigned members executed these Articles of Organization this ___22___ day of __March,_____, __2003___ .

Bill Williams
_____
Member: Bill Williams   Address:
123 Liberty Street, Libertyville, FL 33757

John Johnson
_____
Member: John Johnson   Address:
321 Galt Street, Libertyville, FL 33757

_____
Member: Address:

_____
Member: Address:

Acceptance of registered (statutory) agent

Having been named as registered agent and to accept service of process for the above stated limited liability company at the place designated in this certificate, I hereby accept the appointment as registered agent and agree to act in this capacity. I further agree to comply with the provisions of all statutes relating to the proper and complete performance of my duties, and am familiar with and accept the obligations of my position as registered agent.

Bill Williams
_____
Agent: Bill Williams

Form **SS-4**

(Rev. December 2001)

Department of the Treasury
Internal Revenue Service

Application for Employer Identification Number

(For use by employers, corporations, partnerships, trusts, estates, churches, government agencies, Indian tribal entities, certain individuals, and others.)

· See separate instructions for each line.   · Keep a copy for your records.

EIN

OMB No. 1545-0003

Type or print clearly.

1 Legal name of entity (or individual) for whom the EIN is being requested	
Williams and Johnson, L.L.C.	

2 Trade name of business (if different from name on line 1)	**3** Executor, trustee, "care of" name

4a Mailing address (room, apt., suite no. and street, or P.O. box)	**5a** Street address (if different) (Do not enter a P.O. box.)
123 Liberty Street	
4b City, state, and ZIP code	**5b** City, state, and ZIP code
Libertyville, FL 33757	

6 County and state where principal business is located
Liberty County, FL

7a Name of principal officer, general partner, grantor, owner, or trustor	**7b** SSN, ITIN, or EIN
Bill Williams	123-45-6789

8a Type of entity (check only one box)

- [ ] Sole proprietor (SSN) _____
- [ ] Partnership
- [ ] Corporation (enter form number to be filed) · _____
- [ ] Personal service corp.
- [ ] Church or church-controlled organization
- [ ] Other nonprofit organization (specify) · _____
- [X] Other (specify) · LLC

- [ ] Estate (SSN of decedent) _____
- [ ] Plan administrator (SSN) _____
- [ ] Trust (SSN of grantor) _____
- [ ] National Guard   [ ] State/local government
- [ ] Farmers' cooperative   [ ] Federal government/military
- [ ] REMIC   [ ] Indian tribal governments/enterprises
- Group Exemption Number (GEN) · _____

8b If a corporation, name the state or foreign country (if applicable) where incorporated

State	Foreign country

9 Reason for applying (check only one box)

- [X] Started new business (specify type) · _____
      clothing manufacturer
- [ ] Hired employees (Check the box and see line 12.)
- [ ] Compliance with IRS withholding regulations
- [ ] Other (specify) ·

- [ ] Banking purpose (specify purpose) · _____
- [ ] Changed type of organization (specify new type) · _____
- [ ] Purchased going business
- [ ] Created a trust (specify type) · _____
- [ ] Created a pension plan (specify type) · _____

10 Date business started or acquired (month, day, year)	**11** Closing month of accounting year
10-07-2003	December

12 First date wages or annuities were paid or will be paid (month, day, year). **Note:** *If applicant is a withholding agent, enter date income will first be paid to nonresident alien. (month, day, year)* · · · · · · · · · · · · 10-22-2003

13 Highest number of employees expected in the next 12 months. **Note:** *If the applicant does not expect to have any employees during the period, enter "-0-."* · · · · · · · · · · · ·

Agricultural	Household	Other
0	0	2

14 Check **one** box that best describes the principal activity of your business.
- [ ] Construction [ ] Rental & leasing [ ] Transportation & warehousing [ ] Health care & social assistance [ ] Wholesale–agent/broker
- [ ] Real estate [X] Manufacturing [ ] Finance & insurance [ ] Accommodation & food service [ ] Wholesale–other [ ] Retail
-     [ ] Other (specify)

15 Indicate principal line of merchandise sold; specific construction work done; products produced; or services provided.
clothing manufacturer

16a Has the applicant ever applied for an employer identification number for this or any other business? · · · · · [ ] Yes [X] No
Note: *If "Yes," please complete lines 16b and 16c.*

16b If you checked "Yes" on line 16a, give applicant's legal name and trade name shown on prior application if different from line 1 or 2 above.
Legal name ·   Trade name ·

16c Approximate date when, and city and state where, the application was filed. Enter previous employer identification number if known.

Approximate date when filed (mo., day, year)	City and state where filed	Previous EIN

Third Party Designee	Complete this section **only** if you want to authorize the named individual to receive the entity's EIN and answer questions about the completion of this form.	
	Designee's name	Designee's telephone number (include area code) ( )
	Address and ZIP code	Designee's fax number (include area code) ( )

Under penalties of perjury, I declare that I have examined this application, and to the best of my knowledge and belief, it is true, correct, and complete.

Name and title (type or print clearly) · Bill Williams, Partner

Applicant's telephone number (include area code)
(518) 555-0000

Signature · *Bill Williams*   Date · 10/15/2003

Applicant's fax number (include area code)
(518) 555-0001

For Privacy Act and Paperwork Reduction Act Notice, see separate instructions.   Cat. No. 16055N   Form **SS-4** (Rev. 12-2001)

form 4

Form **8832**

(Rev. September 2002)
Department of the Treasury
Internal Revenue Service

Entity Classification Election

OMB No. 1545-1516

Type or Print	Name of entity Williams and Johnson, L.L.C.

EIN ▶ 59-: 12345678

Number, street, and room or suite no. If a P.O. box, see instructions.
123 Liberty Street

City or town, state, and ZIP code. If a foreign address, enter city, province or state, postal code and country.
Libertyville, FL 33757

1 Type of election (see instructions):

a ☒ Initial classification by a newly-formed entity.

b ☐ Change in current classification.

2 Form of entity (see instructions):

a ☐ A domestic eligible entity electing to be classified as an association taxable as a corporation.

b ☒ A domestic eligible entity electing to be classified as a partnership.

c ☐ A domestic eligible entity with a single owner electing to be disregarded as a separate entity.

d ☐ A foreign eligible entity electing to be classified as an association taxable as a corporation.

e ☐ A foreign eligible entity electing to be classified as a partnership.

f ☐ A foreign eligible entity with a single owner electing to be disregarded as a separate entity.

3 Disregarded entity information (see instructions):
a Name of owner ▶ ....
b Identifying number of owner ▶ ....
c Country of organization of entity electing to be disregarded (if foreign) ▶ ....

4 Election is to be effective beginning (month, day, year) (see instructions) . . . . ▶ ___/___/___

5 Name and title of person whom the IRS may call for more information

Bill Williams

6 That person's telephone number

(909) 555-1212

Consent Statement and Signature(s) (see instructions)

Under penalties of perjury, I (we) declare that I (we) consent to the election of the above-named entity to be classified as indicated above, and that I (we) have examined this consent statement, and to the best of my (our) knowledge and belief, it is true, correct, and complete. If I am an officer, manager, or member signing for all members of the entity, I further declare that I am authorized to execute this consent statement on their behalf.

Signature(s)	Date	Title
Bill Williams	*Oct. 15, 2003*	Member
John Johnson	*Oct. 15, 2003*	Member

For Paperwork Reduction Act Notice, see page 4.   Cat. No. 22598R   Form **8832** (Rev. 9-2002)

Bill of Sale

The undersigned, in consideration of membership interest in __Galt Industries,__

__L.L.C._____, a __Colorado_____ limited liability company,

hereby grants, bargains, sells, transfers and delivers unto said corporation the following goods

and chattels:

    A 1997 Ford panel truck, VIN 1234567890 valued at $12,600
    a G&R industrial lathe, Model 605 valued at $2,800

To have and to hold the same forever.

And the undersigned, their heirs, successors and administrators, covenant and warrant that
they are the lawful owners of the said goods and chattels and that they are free from all
encumbrances. That the undersigned have the right to sell this property and that they will warrant and defend the sale of said property against the lawful claims and demands of all persons.
IN WITNESS whereof the undersigned have executed this Bill of Sale this __1__ day of
__MAY_____, __2003__.

_____*John Galt*_____
       John Galt

_____

_____

Schedule A to
Limited Liability Company
Operating or Management Agreement of
Williams and Johnson, L.L.C.

1. Initial member(s): The initial member(s) are:

   Bill Williams, 123 Liberty Street, Libertyville, SU 90999

   John Johnson, 321 Galt Street, Libertyville, SU 90999

2. Capital Contribution(s): The capital contribution(s) of the member(s) is/are:

   Bill Williams, $5,000 cash

   John Johnson, $2,000 cash, 1992 GMC truck valued at $3,000

3. Profits and Losses: The profits, losses and other tax matters shall be allocated among the members in the following percentages:

   Bill Williams, 50%
   John Johnson, 50%

4. Management. The company shall be managed by:

   Bill Williams, 123 Liberty Street, Libertyville, SU 90999

   John Johnson, 321 Galt Street, Libertyville, SU 90999

5. Registered Agent: the initial registered agent and registered office of the company are:

   Bill Williams, 123 Liberty Street, Libertyville, SU 90999

6. The tax matters partner is:

   Bill Williams

Minutes of a Meeting of Members of

Williams and Johnson, L.L.C.

A meeting of the members of the company was held on _____ May 2, 2003 _____, at
123 Liberty Street, Libertyville, FL 33757 _____.

The following were present, being all the members of the limited liability company:
Bill Williams   John Johnson

The meeting was called to order and it was moved, seconded and unanimously carried that
Bill Williams _____ act as Chairman and that _____ John Johnson _____ act
as Secretary.

After discussion and upon motion duly made, seconded and carried the following resolution(s)
were adopted:

The company agreed to buy a warehouse on Highway 31 in Libertyville
and to finance it it with a loan of $120,000 borrowed from Liberty
Bank at 9% interest payable over 20 years.

There being no further business to come before the meeting, upon motion duly made,
seconded and unanimously carried, it was adjourned.

_____ *John Johnson* _____
Secretary

Members:

Bill Williams

John Johnson

Certificate of Authority

for

Williams and Johnson, L.L.C.

This is to certify that the above limited liability company is managed by its

☒ members

❏ managers

who are listed below and that each of them is authorized and empowered to transact business on behalf of the company.

Name	Address
Bill Williams	123 Liberty Street
	Libertyville, SU 90999
John Johnson	321 Galt Street
	Libertyville, SU 90999

Date: May 29, 2003

Name of company:
Williams and Johnson, L.L.C.

By: *Bill Williams*
    Bill Williams

Position: Member

Banking Resolution of

Williams and Johnson, L.L.C.

The undersigned, being a member of the above limited liability company authorized to sigh this resolution, hereby certifies that on the __6__ day of ____June,____ , __2003__ the members of the limited liability company adopted the following resolution:

RESOLVED that the limited liability company open bank accounts with ____Liberty Bank____ and that the members of the company are authorized to take such action as is necessary to open such accounts; that the bank's printed form of resolution is hereby adopted and incorporated into these minutes by reference; that any __1__ of the following person(s) shall have signature authority over the account:

Bill Williams   John Johnson

and that said resolution has not been modified or rescinded.

Date: __June 6, 2003__

Bill Williams
Authorized member

Appendix C
Blank Forms

TRANSMITTAL LETTER

To:

Re:

Enclosed is an original and _____ copies of articles of organization for the above-referenced LLC along with a check for $_____ as follows:

       $_____ for filing fee

       $_____ for _____

Please send acknowledgement of receipt and/or date-stamped copy to:

This page intentionally left blank.

ARTICLES OF ORGANIZATION FOR A LIMITED LIABILITY COMPANY

ARTICLE I - Name:

The name of the Limited Liability Company is:

ARTICLE II - Purpose:

The purpose for which this limited liability company is organized is:

ARTICLE III - Duration:

The period of duration for the Limited Liability Company shall be:

ARTICLE IV - Registered (or Statutory) Agent and Address:

The name and address of the initial registered (statutory) agent is:

ARTICLE V - Management:
(Check the appropriate box and complete the statement)

☐ The Limited Liability Company is to be managed by a manager or managers and the name(s) and address(es) of such manager(s) who is/are to serve as manager(s) is/are:

☐ The Limited Liability Company is to be managed by the members and the name(s) and address(es) of the managing members is/are:

ARTICLE VI - Principal Place of Business

The initial principal place of business of the limited liability company is:

ARTICLE VII - Effective Date

The effective date of these articles is ☐ upon filing ☐ on _____

ARTICLE VIII - Nonliability

The members and managers, if any, shall not be liable for any debts, obligations or liabilities of the limited liability company.

ARTICLE IX - Miscellaneous

IN WITNESS WHEREOF the undersigned members executed these Articles of Organization this _____ day of _____, _____.

_____

Member: Address:

_____

Member: Address:

_____

Member: Address:

_____

Member: Address:

Acceptance of registered (statutory) agent

Having been named as registered agent and to accept service of process for the above stated limited liability company at the place designated in this certificate, I hereby accept the appointment as registered agent and agree to act in this capacity. I further agree to comply with the provisions of all statutes relating to the proper and complete performance of my duties, and am familiar with and accept the obligations of my position as registered agent.

_____

Agent:

Form **SS-4**

(Rev. December 2001)

Department of the Treasury
Internal Revenue Service

Application for Employer Identification Number

(For use by employers, corporations, partnerships, trusts, estates, churches, government agencies, Indian tribal entities, certain individuals, and others.)

· See separate instructions for each line.   · Keep a copy for your records.

EIN

OMB No. 1545-0003

Type or print clearly.

1 Legal name of entity (or individual) for whom the EIN is being requested

2 Trade name of business (if different from name on line 1)

3 Executor, trustee, "care of" name

4a Mailing address (room, apt., suite no. and street, or P.O. box)

5a Street address (if different) (Do not enter a P.O. box.)

4b City, state, and ZIP code

5b City, state, and ZIP code

6 County and state where principal business is located

7a Name of principal officer, general partner, grantor, owner, or trustor

7b SSN, ITIN, or EIN

8a **Type of entity** (check only one box)

☐ Sole proprietor (SSN) _____

☐ Partnership

☐ Corporation (enter form number to be filed) · _____

☐ Personal service corp.

☐ Church or church-controlled organization

☐ Other nonprofit organization (specify) · _____

☐ Other (specify) · _____

☐ Estate (SSN of decedent) _____

☐ Plan administrator (SSN) _____

☐ Trust (SSN of grantor) _____

☐ National Guard   ☐ State/local government

☐ Farmers' cooperative   ☐ Federal government/military

☐ REMIC   ☐ Indian tribal governments/enterprises

Group Exemption Number (GEN) · _____

8b If a corporation, name the state or foreign country (if applicable) where incorporated

State

Foreign country

9 **Reason for applying** (check only one box)

☐ Started new business (specify type) · _____

☐ Hired employees (Check the box and see line 12.)

☐ Compliance with IRS withholding regulations

☐ Other (specify) · _____

☐ Banking purpose (specify purpose) · _____

☐ Changed type of organization (specify new type) · _____

☐ Purchased going business

☐ Created a trust (specify type) · _____

☐ Created a pension plan (specify type) · _____

10 Date business started or acquired (month, day, year)

11 Closing month of accounting year

12 First date wages or annuities were paid or will be paid (month, day, year). **Note:** *If applicant is a withholding agent, enter date income will first be paid to nonresident alien. (month, day, year)* . . . . ·

13 Highest number of employees expected in the next 12 months. **Note:** *If the applicant does not expect to have any employees during the period, enter "-0-."* . . . . ·

Agricultural	Household	Other

14 Check **one** box that best describes the principal activity of your business.   ☐ Health care & social assistance   ☐ Wholesale–agent/broker

☐ Construction   ☐ Rental & leasing   ☐ Transportation & warehousing   ☐ Accommodation & food service   ☐ Wholesale–other   ☐ Retail

☐ Real estate   ☐ Manufacturing   ☐ Finance & insurance   ☐ Other (specify)

15 Indicate principal line of merchandise sold; specific construction work done; products produced; or services provided.

16a Has the applicant ever applied for an employer identification number for this or any other business? . . . . . ☐ **Yes**   ☐ **No**

Note: *If "Yes," please complete lines 16b and 16c.*

16b If you checked "Yes" on line 16a, give applicant's legal name and trade name shown on prior application if different from line 1 or 2 above.

Legal name ·

Trade name ·

16c Approximate date when, and city and state where, the application was filed. Enter previous employer identification number if known.

Approximate date when filed (mo., day, year)

City and state where filed

Previous EIN

Third Party Designee	Complete this section **only** if you want to authorize the named individual to receive the entity's EIN and answer questions about the completion of this form.	
	Designee's name	Designee's telephone number (include area code) ( )
	Address and ZIP code	Designee's fax number (include area code) ( )

Under penalties of perjury, I declare that I have examined this application, and to the best of my knowledge and belief, it is true, correct, and complete.

Applicant's telephone number (include area code) (   )

Name and title (type or print clearly) ·

Applicant's fax number (include area code) (   )

Signature ·

Date ·

For Privacy Act and Paperwork Reduction Act Notice, see separate instructions.   Cat. No. 16055N   Form **SS-4** (Rev. 12-2001)

Instructions for Form SS-4

(Rev. December 2001)

Application for Employer Identification Number

Section references are to the Internal Revenue Code unless otherwise noted.

General Instructions

Use these instructions to complete **Form SS-4,** Application for Employer Identification Number. Also see **Do I Need an EIN?** on page 2 of Form SS-4.

Purpose of Form

Use Form SS-4 to apply for an employer identification number (EIN). An EIN is a nine-digit number (for example, 12-3456789) assigned to sole proprietors, corporations, partnerships, estates, trusts, and other entities for tax filing and reporting purposes. The information you provide on this form will establish your business tax account.

 *An EIN is for use in connection with your business activities only. Do **not** use your EIN in place of your social security number (SSN).*

File only one Form SS-4. Generally, a sole proprietor should file only one Form SS-4 and needs only one EIN, regardless of the number of businesses operated as a sole proprietorship or trade names under which a business operates. However, if the proprietorship incorporates or enters into a partnership, a new EIN is required. Also, each corporation in an affiliated group must have its own EIN.

EIN applied for, but not received. If you do not have an EIN by the time a **return** is due, write "Applied For" and the date you applied in the space shown for the number. **Do not** show your social security number (SSN) as an EIN on returns.

If you do not have an EIN by the time a **tax deposit** is due, send your payment to the Internal Revenue Service Center for your filing area as shown in the instructions for the form that you are are filing. Make your check or money order payable to the **"United States Treasury"** and show your name (as shown on Form SS-4), address, type of tax, period covered, and date you applied for an EIN.

Related Forms and Publications

The following **forms** and **instructions** may be useful to filers of Form SS-4:
- **Form 990-T,** Exempt Organization Business Income Tax Return
- **Instructions for Form 990-T**
- **Schedule C (Form 1040),** Profit or Loss From Business
- **Schedule F (Form 1040),** Profit or Loss From Farming
- **Instructions for Form 1041 and Schedules A, B, D, G, I, J, and K-1,** U.S. Income Tax Return for Estates and Trusts

- **Form 1042,** Annual Withholding Tax Return for U.S. Source Income of Foreign Persons
- **Instructions for Form 1065,** U.S. Return of Partnership Income
- **Instructions for Form 1066,** U.S. Real Estate Mortgage Investment Conduit (REMIC) Income Tax Return
- **Instructions for Forms 1120 and 1120-A**
- **Form 2553,** Election by a Small Business Corporation
- **Form 2848,** Power of Attorney and Declaration of Representative
- **Form 8821,** Tax Information Authorization
- **Form 8832,** Entity Classification Election

For more **information** about filing Form SS-4 and related issues, see:
- **Circular A,** Agricultural Employer's Tax Guide (Pub. 51)
- **Circular E,** Employer's Tax Guide (Pub. 15)
- **Pub. 538,** Accounting Periods and Methods
- **Pub. 542,** Corporations
- **Pub. 557,** Exempt Status for Your Organization
- **Pub. 583,** Starting a Business and Keeping Records
- **Pub. 966,** EFTPS: Now a Full Range of Electronic Choices to Pay All Your Federal Taxes
- **Pub. 1635,** Understanding Your EIN
- **Package 1023,** Application for Recognition of Exemption
- **Package 1024,** Application for Recognition of Exemption Under Section 501(a)

How To Get Forms and Publications

Phone. You can order forms, instructions, and publications by phone 24 hours a day, 7 days a week. Just call 1-800-TAX-FORM (1-800-829-3676). You should receive your order or notification of its status within 10 workdays.

Personal computer. With your personal computer and modem, you can get the forms and information you need using the IRS Web Site at **www.irs.gov** or File Transfer Protocol at **ftp.irs.gov.**

CD-ROM. For small businesses, return preparers, or others who may frequently need tax forms or publications, a CD-ROM containing over 2,000 tax products (including many prior year forms) can be purchased from the National Technical Information Service (NTIS).

To order **Pub. 1796,** Federal Tax Products on CD-ROM, call **1-877-CDFORMS** (1-877-233-6767) toll free or connect to **www.irs.gov/cdorders.**

Tax Help for Your Business

IRS-sponsored Small Business Workshops provide information about your Federal and state tax obligations. For information about workshops in your area, call 1-800-829-1040 and ask for your Taxpayer Education Coordinator.

How To Apply

You can apply for an EIN by telephone, fax, or mail depending on how soon you need to use the EIN.

Application by Tele-TIN. Under the Tele-TIN program, you can receive your EIN by telephone and use it immediately to file a return or make a payment. To receive an EIN by telephone, IRS suggests that you complete Form SS-4 so that you will have all relevant information available. Then call the Tele-TIN number at 1-866-816-2065. (International applicants must call 215-516-6999.) Tele-TIN hours of operation are 7:30 a.m. to 5:30 p.m. The person making the call must be authorized to sign the form or be an authorized designee. See **Signature** and **Third Party Designee** on page 6. Also see the **TIP** below.

An IRS representative will use the information from the Form SS-4 to establish your account and assign you an EIN. Write the number you are given on the upper right corner of the form and sign and date it. Keep this copy for your records.

If requested by an IRS representative, mail or fax (facsimile) the signed Form SS-4 (including any Third Party Designee authorization) **within 24 hours** to the Tele-TIN Unit at the service center address provided by the IRS representative.

 *Taxpayer representatives can use Tele-TIN to apply for an EIN on behalf of their client and request that the EIN be faxed to their **client** on the same day. (**Note:** By utilizing this procedure, you are authorizing the IRS to fax the EIN without a cover sheet.)*

Application by Fax-TIN. Under the Fax-TIN program, you can receive your EIN by fax within 4 business days. Complete and fax Form SS-4 to the IRS using the Fax-TIN number listed below for your state. A long-distance charge to callers outside of the local calling area will apply. Fax-TIN numbers can only be used to apply for an EIN. **The numbers may change without notice.** Fax-TIN is available 24 hours a day, 7 days a week.

Be sure to provide your fax number so that IRS can fax the EIN back to you. (**Note:** By utilizing this procedure, you are authorizing the IRS to fax the EIN without a cover sheet.)

Do not call Tele-TIN for the same entity because duplicate EINs may be issued. See **Third Party Designee** on page 6.

Application by mail. Complete Form SS-4 at least 4 to 5 weeks before you will need an EIN. Sign and date the application and mail it to the service center address for your state. You will receive your EIN in the mail in approximately 4 weeks. See also **Third Party Designee** on page 6.

Call 1-800-829-1040 to verify a number or to ask about the status of an application by mail.

If your principal business, office or agency, or legal residence in the case of an individual, is located in:	Call the Tele-TIN or Fax-TIN number shown or file with the "Internal Revenue Service Center" at:
Connecticut, Delaware, District of Columbia, Florida, Georgia, Maine, Maryland, Massachusetts, New Hampshire, New Jersey, New York, North Carolina, Ohio, Pennsylvania, Rhode Island, South Carolina, Vermont, Virginia, West Virginia	Attn: EIN Operation Holtsville, NY 00501 Tele-TIN 866-816-2065 Fax-TIN 631-447-8960
Illinois, Indiana, Kentucky, Michigan	Attn: EIN Operation Cincinnati, OH 45999 Tele-TIN 866-816-2065 Fax-TIN 859-669-5760
Alabama, Alaska, Arizona, Arkansas, California, Colorado, Hawaii, Idaho, Iowa, Kansas, Louisiana, Minnesota, Mississippi, Missouri, Montana, Nebraska, Nevada, New Mexico, North Dakota, Oklahoma, Oregon, Puerto Rico, South Dakota, Tennessee, Texas, Utah, Washington, Wisconsin, Wyoming	Attn: EIN Operation Philadelphia, PA 19255 Tele-TIN 866-816-2065 Fax-TIN 215-516-3990
If you have no legal residence, principal place of business, or principal office or agency in any state:	Attn: EIN Operation Philadelphia, PA 19255 Tele-TIN 215-516-6999 Fax-TIN 215-516-3990

Specific Instructions

Print or type all entries on Form SS-4. Follow the instructions for each line to expedite processing and to avoid unnecessary IRS requests for additional information. Enter "N/A" (nonapplicable) on the lines that do not apply.

Line 1—Legal name of entity (or individual) for whom the EIN is being requested. Enter the legal name of the entity (or individual) applying for the EIN exactly as it appears on the social security card, charter, or other applicable legal document.

Individuals. Enter your first name, middle initial, and last name. If you are a sole proprietor, enter your individual name, not your business name. Enter your business name on line 2. Do not use abbreviations or nicknames on line 1.

Trusts. Enter the name of the trust.

Estate of a decedent. Enter the name of the estate.

Partnerships. Enter the legal name of the partnership as it appears in the partnership agreement.

Corporations. Enter the corporate name as it appears in the corporation charter or other legal document creating it.

Plan administrators. Enter the name of the plan administrator. A plan administrator who already has an EIN should use that number.

Line 2—Trade name of business. Enter the trade name of the business if different from the legal name. The trade name is the "doing business as " (DBA) name.

 *Use the full legal name shown on line 1 on all tax returns filed for the entity. (However, if you enter a trade name on line 2 and choose to use the trade name instead of the legal name, enter the trade name on **all returns** you file.) To prevent processing delays and errors, **always** use the legal name only (or the trade name only) on **all** tax returns.*

Line 3—Executor, trustee, "care of" name. Trusts enter the name of the trustee. Estates enter the name of the executor, administrator, or other fiduciary. If the entity applying has a designated person to receive tax information, enter that person's name as the "care of" person. Enter the individual's first name, middle initial, and last name.

Lines 4a-b—Mailing address. Enter the mailing address for the entity's correspondence. If line 3 is completed, enter the address for the executor, trustee or "care of" person. Generally, this address will be used on all tax returns.

TIP *File **Form 8822**, Change of Address, to report any subsequent changes to the entity's mailing address.*

Lines 5a-b—Street address. Provide the entity's physical address **only** if different from its mailing address shown in lines 4a-b. **Do not** enter a P.O. box number here.

Line 6—County and state where principal business is located. Enter the entity's primary **physical** location.

Lines 7a-b—Name of principal officer, general partner, grantor, owner, or trustor. Enter the first name, middle initial, last name, and SSN of **(a)** the principal officer if the business is a corporation, **(b)** a general partner if a partnership, **(c)** the owner of an entity that is disregarded as separate from its owner (disregarded entities owned by a corporation enter the corporation's name and EIN), or **(d)** a grantor, owner, or trustor if a trust.

If the person in question is an **alien individual** with a previously assigned individual taxpayer identification number (ITIN), enter the ITIN in the space provided and submit a copy of an official identifying document. If necessary, complete **Form W-7,** Application for IRS Individual Taxpayer Identification Number, to obtain an ITIN.

You are **required** to enter an SSN, ITIN, or EIN unless the only reason you are applying for an EIN is to make an entity classification election (see Regulations section 301.7701-1 through 301.7701-3) and you are a nonresident alien with no effectively connected income from sources within the United States.

Line 8a—Type of entity. Check the box that best describes the type of entity applying for the EIN. If you are an alien individual with an ITIN previously assigned to you, enter the ITIN in place of a requested SSN.

 *This is not an election for a tax classification of an entity. See **"Limited liability company (LLC)"** on page 4.*

Other. If not specifically mentioned, check the "Other" box, enter the type of entity and the type of return, if any, that will be filed (for example, "Common Trust Fund, Form 1065" or "Created a Pension Plan"). Do not enter "N/A." If you are an alien individual applying for an EIN, see the **Lines 7a-b** instructions above.

● **Household employer.** If you are an individual, check the "Other" box and enter "Household Employer" and your SSN. If you are a state or local agency serving as a tax reporting agent for public assistance recipients who become household employers, check the "Other" box and enter "Household Employer Agent." If you are a trust that qualifies as a household employer, you do not need a separate EIN for reporting tax information relating to household employees; use the EIN of the trust.

● **QSub.** For a qualified subchapter S subsidiary (QSub) check the "Other" box and specify "QSub."

● **Withholding agent.** If you are a withholding agent required to file Form 1042, check the "Other" box and enter "Withholding Agent."

Sole proprietor. Check this box if you file Schedule C, C-EZ, or F (Form 1040) and have a qualified plan, or are required to file excise, employment, or alcohol, tobacco, or firearms returns, or are a payer of gambling winnings. Enter your SSN (or ITIN) in the space provided. If you are a nonresident alien with no effectively connected income from sources within the United States, you do not need to enter an SSN or ITIN.

Corporation. This box is for any corporation **other than a personal service corporation.** If you check this box, enter the income tax form number to be filed by the entity in the space provided.

 *If you entered **"1120S"** after the "Corporation" checkbox, the corporation **must** file Form 2553 **no later than the 15th day of the 3rd month of the tax year the election is to take effect.** Until Form 2553 has been received and approved, you will be considered a Form 1120 filer. See the Instructions for Form 2553.*

Personal service corp. Check this box if the entity is a personal service corporation. An entity is a personal service corporation for a tax year only if:
● The principal activity of the entity during the testing period (prior tax year) for the tax year is the performance of personal services substantially by employee-owners, and
● The employee-owners own at least 10% of the fair market value of the outstanding stock in the entity on the last day of the testing period.

Personal services include performance of services in such fields as health, law, accounting, or consulting. For more information about personal service corporations, see the Instructions for Forms 1120 and 1120-A and Pub. 542.

Other nonprofit organization. Check this box if the nonprofit organization is other than a church or church-controlled organization and specify the type of nonprofit organization (for example, an educational organization).

 *If the organization also seeks tax-exempt status, you **must** file either Package 1023 or Package 1024. See Pub. 557 for more information.*

If the organization is covered by a group exemption letter, enter the four-digit **group exemption number (GEN).** (Do not confuse the GEN with the nine-digit EIN.) If you do not know the GEN, contact the parent organization. Get Pub. 557 for more information about group exemption numbers.

Plan administrator. If the plan administrator is an individual, enter the plan administrator's SSN in the space provided.

REMIC. Check this box if the entity has elected to be treated as a real estate mortgage investment conduit (REMIC). See the Instructions for Form 1066 for more information.

Limited liability company (LLC). An LLC is an entity organized under the laws of a state or foreign country as a limited liability company. For Federal tax purposes, an LLC may be treated as a partnership or corporation or be disregarded as an entity separate from its owner.

By **default,** a domestic LLC with only one member is **disregarded** as an entity separate from its owner and must include all of its income and expenses on the owner's tax return (e.g., **Schedule C (Form 1040)**). Also by default, a domestic LLC with two or more members is treated as a partnership. A domestic LLC may file Form 8832 to avoid either default classification and elect to be classified as an association taxable as a corporation. For more information on entity classifications (including the rules for foreign entities), see the instructions for Form 8832.

 Do not** file Form 8832 if the LLC accepts the default classifications above. **However, if the LLC will be electing S Corporation status, it must timely file both Form 8832 and Form 2553.

Complete Form SS-4 for LLCs as follows:
• A single-member, domestic LLC that accepts the default classification (above) does not need an EIN and generally should not file Form SS-4. Generally, the LLC should use the name and EIN of its **owner** for all Federal tax purposes. However, the reporting and payment of employment taxes for employees of the LLC may be made using the name and EIN or **either** the owner or the LLC as explained in Notice 99-6, 1999-1 C.B. 321. You can find Notice 99-6 on page 12 of Internal Revenue Bulletin 1999-3 at **www.irs.gov. (Note:** If the LLC-applicant indicates in box 13 that it has employees or expects to have employees, the owner (whether an individual or other entity) of a single-member domestic LLC will also be assigned its own EIN (if it does not

already have one) even if the LLC will be filing the employment tax returns.)
• A single-member, domestic LLC that accepts the default classification (above) and wants an EIN for filing employment tax returns (see above) or non-Federal purposes, such as a state requirement, must check the "Other" box and write "Disregarded Entity" or, when applicable, "Disregarded Entity—Sole Proprietorship" in the space provided.
• A multi-member, domestic LLC that accepts the default classification (above) must check the "Partnership" box.
• A domestic LLC that will be filing Form 8832 to elect corporate status must check the "Corporation" box and write in "Single-Member" or "Multi-Member" immediately below the "form number" entry line.

Line 9—Reason for applying. Check only **one** box. Do not enter "N/A."

Started new business. Check this box if you are starting a new business that requires an EIN. If you check this box, enter the type of business being started. **Do not** apply if you already have an EIN and are only adding another place of business.

Hired employees. Check this box if the existing business is requesting an EIN because it has hired or is hiring employees and is therefore required to file employment tax returns. **Do not** apply if you already have an EIN and are only hiring employees. For information on employment taxes (e.g., for family members), see Circular E.

 You may be required to make electronic deposits of all depository taxes (such as employment tax, excise tax, and corporate income tax) using the Electronic Federal Tax Payment System (EFTPS). See section 11, Depositing Taxes, of Circular E and Pub. 966.

Created a pension plan. Check this box if you have created a pension plan and need an EIN for reporting purposes. Also, enter the type of plan in the space provided.

 Check this box if you are applying for a trust EIN when a new pension plan is established. In addition, check the "Other" box in line 8a and write "Created a Pension Plan" in the space provided.

Banking purpose. Check this box if you are requesting an EIN for banking purposes only, and enter the banking purpose (for example, a bowling league for depositing dues or an investment club for dividend and interest reporting).

Changed type of organization. Check this box if the business is changing its type of organization for example, the business was a sole proprietorship and has been incorporated or has become a partnership. If you check this box, specify in the space provided (including available space immediately below) the type of change made. For example, "From Sole Proprietorship to Partnership."

Purchased going business. Check this box if you purchased an existing business. **Do not** use the former owner's EIN unless you became the "owner" of a corporation by acquiring its stock.

149

Created a trust. Check this box if you created a trust, and enter the type of trust created. For example, indicate if the trust is a nonexempt charitable trust or a split-interest trust.

Exception. Do **not** file this form for certain grantor-type trusts. The trustee does not need an EIN for the trust if the trustee furnishes the name and TIN of the grantor/owner and the address of the trust to all payors. See the Instructions for Form 1041 for more information.

 Do not check this box if you are applying for a trust EIN when a new pension plan is established. Check "Created a pension plan."

Other. Check this box if you are requesting an EIN for any other reason; and enter the reason. For example, a newly-formed state government entity should enter "Newly-Formed State Government Entity" in the space provided.

Line 10—Date business started or acquired. If you are starting a new business, enter the starting date of the business. If the business you acquired is already operating, enter the date you acquired the business. Trusts should enter the date the trust was legally created. Estates should enter the date of death of the decedent whose name appears on line 1 or the date when the estate was legally funded.

Line 11—Closing month of accounting year. Enter the last month of your accounting year or tax year. An accounting or tax year is usually 12 consecutive months, either a calendar year or a fiscal year (including a period of 52 or 53 weeks). A calendar year is 12 consecutive months ending on December 31. A fiscal year is either 12 consecutive months ending on the last day of any month other than December or a 52-53 week year. For more information on accounting periods, see Pub. 538.

Individuals. Your tax year generally will be a calendar year.

Partnerships. Partnerships must adopt one of the following tax years:
- The tax year of the majority of its partners,
- The tax year common to all of its principal partners,
- The tax year that results in the least aggregate deferral of income, or
- In certain cases, some other tax year.
    See the Instructions for Form 1065 for more information.

REMICs. REMICs must have a calendar year as their tax year.

Personal service corporations. A personal service corporation generally must adopt a calendar year unless:
- It can establish a business purpose for having a different tax year, or
- It elects under section 444 to have a tax year other than a calendar year.

Trusts. Generally, a trust must adopt a calendar year except for the following:
- Tax-exempt trusts,
- Charitable trusts, and
- Grantor-owned trusts.

Line 12—First date wages or annuities were paid or will be paid. If the business has or will have employees, enter the date on which the business began or will begin to pay wages. If the business does not plan to have employees, enter "N/A."

Withholding agent. Enter the date you began or will begin to pay income (including annuities) to a nonresident alien. This also applies to individuals who are required to file Form 1042 to report alimony paid to a nonresident alien.

Line 13—Highest number of employees expected in the next 12 months. Complete each box by entering the number (including zero ("-0-")) of "Agricultural," "Household," or "Other" employees expected by the applicant in the next 12 months. For a definition of agricultural labor (farmwork), see Circular A.

Lines 14 and 15. Check the **one** box in line 14 that best describes the principal activity of the applicant's business. Check the "Other" box (and specify the applicant's principal activity) if none of the listed boxes applies.

Use line 15 to describe the applicant's principal line of business in more detail. For example, if you checked the "Construction" box in line 14, enter additional detail such as "General contractor for residential buildings" in line 15.

 Do not complete lines 14 and 15 if you entered zero "(-0-)" in line 13.

Construction. Check this box if the applicant is engaged in erecting buildings or other structures, (e.g., streets, highways, bridges, tunnels). The term "Construction" also includes special trade contractors, (e.g., plumbing, HVAC, electrical, carpentry, concrete, excavation, etc. contractors).

Real estate. Check this box if the applicant is engaged in renting or leasing real estate to others; managing, selling, buying or renting real estate for others; or providing related real estate services (e.g., appraisal services).

Rental and leasing. Check this box if the applicant is engaged in providing tangible goods such as autos, computers, consumer goods, or industrial machinery and equipment to customers in return for a periodic rental or lease payment.

Manufacturing. Check this box if the applicant is engaged in the mechanical, physical, or chemical transformation of materials, substances, or components into new products. The assembling of component parts of manufactured products is also considered to be manufacturing.

Transportation & warehousing. Check this box if the applicant provides transportation of passengers or cargo; warehousing or storage of goods; scenic or sight-seeing transportation; or support activities related to these modes of transportation.

Finance & insurance. Check this box if the applicant is engaged in transactions involving the creation, liquidation, or change of ownership of financial assets and/or facilitating such financial transactions;

150

underwriting annuities/insurance policies; facilitating such underwriting by selling insurance policies; or by providing other insurance or employee-benefit related services.

Health care and social assistance. Check this box if the applicant is engaged in providing physical, medical, or psychiatric care using licensed health care professionals or providing social assistance activities such as youth centers, adoption agencies, individual/family services, temporary shelters, etc.

Accommodation & food services. Check this box if the applicant is engaged in providing customers with lodging, meal preparation, snacks, or beverages for immediate consumption.

Wholesale–agent/broker. Check this box if the applicant is engaged in arranging for the purchase or sale of goods owned by others or purchasing goods on a commission basis for goods traded in the wholesale market, usually between businesses.

Wholesale–other. Check this box if the applicant is engaged in selling goods in the wholesale market generally to other businesses for resale on their own account.

Retail. Check this box if the applicant is engaged in selling merchandise to the general public from a fixed store; by direct, mail-order, or electronic sales; or by using vending machines.

Other. Check this box if the applicant is engaged in an activity not described above. Describe the applicant's principal business activity in the space provided.

Lines 16a-c. Check the applicable box in line 16a to indicate whether or not the entity (or individual) applying for an EIN was issued one previously. Complete lines 16b and 16c **only** if the "Yes" box in line 16a is checked. If the applicant previously applied for **more than one** EIN, write "See Attached" in the empty space in line 16a and attach a separate sheet providing the line 16b and 16c information for each EIN previously requested.

Third Party Designee. Complete this section **only** if you want to authorize the named individual to receive the entity's EIN and answer questions about the completion of Form SS-4. The designee's authority terminates at the time the EIN is assigned and released to the designee. **You must complete the signature area for the authorization to be valid.**

Signature. When required, the application must be signed by **(a)** the individual, if the applicant is an individual, **(b)** the president, vice president, or other principal officer, if the applicant is a corporation, **(c)** a responsible and duly authorized member or officer having knowledge of its affairs, if the applicant is a partnership, government entity, or other unincorporated organization, or **(d)** the fiduciary, if the applicant is a trust or an estate. Foreign applicants may have any duly-authorized person, (e.g., division manager), sign Form SS-4.

Privacy Act and Paperwork Reduction Act Notice. We ask for the information on this form to carry out the Internal Revenue laws of the United States. We need it to comply with section 6109 and the regulations thereunder which generally require the inclusion of an employer identification number (EIN) on certain returns, statements, or other documents filed with the Internal Revenue Service. If your entity is required to obtain an EIN, you are required to provide all of the information requested on this form. Information on this form may be used to determine which Federal tax returns you are required to file and to provide you with related forms and publications.

We disclose this form to the Social Security Administration for their use in determining compliance with applicable laws. We may give this information to the Department of Justice for use in civil and criminal litigation, and to the cities, states, and the District of Columbia for use in administering their tax laws. We may also disclose this information to Federal, state, or local agencies that investigate or respond to acts or threats of terrorism or participate in intelligence or counterintelligence activities concerning terrorism.

We will be unable to issue an EIN to you unless you provide all of the requested information which applies to your entity. Providing false information could subject you to penalties.

You are not required to provide the information requested on a form that is subject to the Paperwork Reduction Act unless the form displays a valid OMB control number. Books or records relating to a form or its instructions must be retained as long as their contents may become material in the administration of any Internal Revenue law. Generally, tax returns and return information are confidential, as required by section 6103.

The time needed to complete and file this form will vary depending on individual circumstances. The estimated average time is:

Recordkeeping	6 min.
Learning about the law or the form	22 min.
Preparing the form	46 min.
Copying, assembling, and sending the form to the IRS	20 min.

If you have comments concerning the accuracy of these time estimates or suggestions for making this form simpler, we would be happy to hear from you. You can write to the Tax Forms Committee, Western Area Distribution Center, Rancho Cordova, CA 95743-0001. **Do not** send the form to this address. Instead, see **How To Apply** on page 2.

form 4

Entity Classification Election

OMB No. 1545-1516

Type or Print	Name of entity	EIN ▶
	Number, street, and room or suite no. If a P.O. box, see instructions.	
	City or town, state, and ZIP code. If a foreign address, enter city, province or state, postal code and country.	

1   Type of election (see instructions):

a ☐ Initial classification by a newly-formed entity.

b ☐ Change in current classification.

2   Form of entity (see instructions):

a ☐ A domestic eligible entity electing to be classified as an association taxable as a corporation.

b ☐ A domestic eligible entity electing to be classified as a partnership.

c ☐ A domestic eligible entity with a single owner electing to be disregarded as a separate entity.

d ☐ A foreign eligible entity electing to be classified as an association taxable as a corporation.

e ☐ A foreign eligible entity electing to be classified as a partnership.

f ☐ A foreign eligible entity with a single owner electing to be disregarded as a separate entity.

3   Disregarded entity information (see instructions):
a Name of owner ▶ ....
b Identifying number of owner ▶ ....
c Country of organization of entity electing to be disregarded (if foreign) ▶ ....

4   Election is to be effective beginning (month, day, year) (see instructions) . . . . ▶ ____ / ____ / ____

5 Name and title of person whom the IRS may call for more information	**6** That person's telephone number
	( )

Consent Statement and Signature(s) (see instructions)

Under penalties of perjury, I (we) declare that I (we) consent to the election of the above-named entity to be classified as indicated above, and that I (we) have examined this consent statement, and to the best of my (our) knowledge and belief, it is true, correct, and complete. If I am an officer, manager, or member signing for all members of the entity, I further declare that I am authorized to execute this consent statement on their behalf.

Signature(s)	Date	Title

General Instructions

Section references are to the Internal Revenue Code unless otherwise noted.

Purpose of Form

For Federal tax purposes, certain business entities automatically are classified as corporations. See items **1** and **3** through **8** under the definition of **corporation** on this page. Other business entities may choose how they are classified for Federal tax purposes. Except for a business entity automatically classified as a corporation, a business entity with at least two members can choose to be classified as either an association taxable as a corporation or a partnership, and a business entity with a single member can choose to be classified as either an association taxable as a corporation or disregarded as an entity separate from its owner.

Generally, an eligible entity that does not file this form will be classified under the default rules described below. An eligible entity that chooses not to be classified under the default rules or that wishes to change its current classification must file Form 8832 to elect a classification. The IRS will use the information entered on this form to establish the entity's filing and reporting requirements for Federal tax purposes.

60-month limitation rule. Once an eligible entity makes an election to change its classification, the entity generally cannot change its classification by election again during the 60 months after the effective date of the election. However, the IRS may (**by private letter ruling**) permit the entity to change its classification by election within the 60-month period if more than 50% of the ownership interests in the entity as of the effective date of the election are owned by persons that did not own any interests in the entity on the effective date of the entity's prior election. See Regulations section 301.7701-3(c)(1)(iv) for more details.

Note: *The 60-month limitation does not apply if the previous election was made by a newly formed eligible entity and was effective on the date of formation.*

Default Rules

Existing entity default rule. Certain domestic and foreign entities that were in existence before January 1, 1997, and have an established Federal tax classification generally do not need to make an election to continue that classification. If an existing entity decides to change its classification, it may do so subject to the 60-month limitation rule. See Regulations sections 301.7701-3(b)(3) and 301.7701-3(h)(2) for more details.

Domestic default rule. Unless an election is made on Form 8832, a domestic eligible entity is:

1. A partnership if it has two or more members.

2. Disregarded as an entity separate from its owner if it has a single owner.

A change in the number of members of an eligible entity classified as an association does not affect the entity's classification. However, an eligible entity classified as a partnership will become a disregarded entity when the entity's membership is reduced to one member and a disregarded entity will be classified as a partnership when the entity has more than one member.

Foreign default rule. Unless an election is made on Form 8832, a foreign eligible entity is:

1. A partnership if it has two or more members and **at least** one member does not have limited liability.

2. An association taxable as a corporation if all members have limited liability.

3. Disregarded as an entity separate from its owner if it has a single owner that does not have limited liability.

Definitions

Association. For purposes of this form, an association is an eligible entity that is taxable as a corporation by election or, for foreign eligible entities, under the default rules (see Regulations section 301.7701-3).

Business entity. A business entity is any entity recognized for Federal tax purposes that is not properly classified as a trust under Regulations section 301.7701-4 or otherwise subject to special treatment under the Code. See Regulations section 301.7701-2(a).

Corporation. For Federal tax purposes, a corporation is any of the following:

1. A business entity organized under a Federal or state statute, or under a statute of a federally recognized Indian tribe, if the statute describes or refers to the entity as incorporated or as a corporation, body corporate, or body politic.

2. An association (as determined under Regulations section 301.7701-3).

3. A business entity organized under a state statute, if the statute describes or refers to the entity as a joint-stock company or joint-stock association.

4. An insurance company.

5. A state-chartered business entity conducting banking activities, if any of its deposits are insured under the Federal Deposit Insurance Act, as amended, 12 U.S.C. 1811 et seq., or a similar Federal statute.

6. A business entity wholly owned by a state or any political subdivision thereof, or a business entity wholly owned by a foreign government or any other entity described in Regulations section 1.892-2T.

7. A business entity that is taxable as a corporation under a provision of the Code other than section 7701(a)(3).

8. A foreign business entity listed on page 5. See Regulations section 301.7701-2(b)(8) for any exceptions and inclusions to items on this list and for any revisions made to this list since these instructions were printed.

Disregarded entity. A disregarded entity is an eligible entity that is treated as an entity that is not separate from its single owner. Its separate existence will be ignored for Federal tax purposes unless it elects corporate tax treatment.

Eligible entity. An eligible entity is a business entity that is not included in items **1** or **3** through **8** under the definition of corporation above.

Limited liability. A member of a foreign eligible entity has limited liability if the member has no personal liability for any debts of or claims against the entity by reason of being a member. This determination is based solely on the statute or law under which the entity is organized (and, if relevant, the entity's organizational documents). A member has personal liability if the creditors of the entity may seek satisfaction of all or any part of the debts or claims against the entity from the member as such. A member has personal liability even if the member makes an agreement under which another person (whether or not a member of the entity) assumes that liability or agrees to indemnify that member for that liability.

Partnership. A partnership is a business entity that has **at least** two members and is not a corporation as defined on page 2.

Who Must File

File this form for an **eligible entity** that is one of the following:

● A domestic entity electing to be classified as an association taxable as a corporation.

● A domestic entity electing to change its current classification (even if it is currently classified under the default rule).

● A foreign entity that has more than one owner, all owners having limited liability, electing to be classified as a partnership.

● A foreign entity that has at least one owner that does not have limited liability, electing to be classified as an association taxable as a corporation.

● A foreign entity with a single owner having limited liability, electing to be an entity disregarded as an entity separate from its owner.

● A foreign entity electing to change its current classification (even if it is currently classified under the default rule).

Do not file this form for an eligible entity that is:

● Tax-exempt under section 501(a) or

● A real estate investment trust (REIT), as defined in section 856.

Effect of Election

The Federal tax treatment of elective changes in classification as described in Regulations section 301.7701-3(g)(1) is summarized as follows:

● If an eligible entity classified as a partnership elects to be classified as an association, it is deemed that the partnership contributes all of its assets and liabilities to the association in exchange for stock in the association, and immediately thereafter, the partnership liquidates by distributing the stock of the association to its partners.

● If an eligible entity classified as an association elects to be classified as a partnership, it is deemed that the association distributes all of its assets and liabilities to its shareholders in liquidation of the association, and immediately thereafter, the shareholders contribute all of the distributed assets and liabilities to a newly formed partnership.

● If an eligible entity classified as an association elects to be disregarded as an entity separate from its owner, it is deemed that the association distributes all of its assets and liabilities to its single owner in liquidation of the association.

● If an eligible entity that is disregarded as an entity separate from its owner elects to be classified as an association, the owner of the eligible entity is deemed to have contributed all of the assets and liabilities of the entity to the association in exchange for the stock of the association.

Note: *For information on the Federal tax treatment of elective changes in classification, see Regulations section 301.7701-3(g).*

When To File

See the instructions for line 4.

A newly formed entity may be eligible for late election relief under Rev. Proc. 2002-59, 2002-39 I.R.B. 615 if:

● The entity failed to obtain its desired classified election solely because Form 8832 was not timely filed,

● The due date for the entity's desired classification tax return (excluding extension) for the tax year beginning with the entity's formation date has not passed, and

● The entity has reasonable cause for its failure to make a timely election.

To obtain relief, a newly formed entity must file Form 8832 on or before the due date of the first Federal tax return (excluding extensions) of the entity's desired classification. The entity must also write "FILED PURSUANT TO REV. PROC. 2002-59" at the top of the form. The entity must attach a statement to the form explaining why it failed to file a timely election. If Rev. Proc. 2002-59 does not apply, an entity may seek relief for a late entity election by requesting a private letter ruling and paying a user fee in accordance with Rev. Proc. 2002-1, 2002-1 I.R.B. 1 (or its successor).

Where To File

File Form 8832 with the Internal Revenue Service Center, Philadelphia, PA 19255. Also attach a copy of Form 8832 to the entity's Federal income tax or information return for the tax year of the election. If the entity is not required to file a return for that year, a copy of its Form 8832 **must** be attached to the Federal income tax or information returns of **all** direct or indirect owners of the entity for the tax year of the owner that includes the date on which the election took effect. Although failure to attach a copy will not invalidate an otherwise valid election, each member of the entity is required to file returns that are consistent with the entity's election. In addition, penalties may be assessed against persons who are required to, but who do not, attach Form 8832 to their returns. Other penalties may apply for filing Federal income tax or information returns inconsistent with the entity's election.

Specific Instructions

Name. Enter the name of the eligible entity electing to be classified using Form 8832.

Employer identification number (EIN). Show the correct EIN of the eligible entity electing to be classified. Any entity that has an EIN will retain that EIN even if its Federal tax classification changes under Regulations section 301.7701-3.

If a disregarded entity's classification changes so that it is recognized as a partnership or association for Federal tax purposes, and that entity had an EIN, then the entity must use that EIN and not the identifying number of the single owner. If the entity did not already have its own EIN, then the entity must apply for an EIN and not use the identifying number of the single owner.

A foreign person that makes an election under Regulations section 301.7701-3(c) must also use its own taxpayer identifying number. See sections 6721 through 6724 for penalties that may apply for failure to supply taxpayer identifying numbers.

If the entity electing to be classified using Form 8832 does not have an EIN, it must apply for one on **Form SS-4,** Application for Employer Identification Number. If the filing of Form 8832 is the only reason the entity is applying for an EIN, check the "Other" box on line 9 of Form SS-4 and write "Form 8832" to the right of that box. If the entity has not received an EIN by the time Form 8832 is due, write "Applied for" in the space for the EIN. **Do not** apply for a new EIN for an existing entity that is changing its classification if the entity already has an EIN.

Address. Enter the address of the entity electing a classification. Include the suite, room, or other unit number after the street address. If the Post Office does not deliver mail to the street address and the entity has a P.O. box, show the box number instead of the street address.

Line 1. Check box 1a if the entity is choosing a classification for the first time **and** the entity does not want to be classified under the applicable default classification. **Do not** file this form if the entity wants to be classified under the default rules.

Check box 1b if the entity is changing its current classification.

Line 2. Check the appropriate box if you are changing a current classification (no matter how achieved), or are electing out of a default classification. **Do not** file this form if you fall within a default classification that is the desired classification for the new entity.

Line 3. If an eligible entity has checked box 2c or box 2f and is electing to be disregarded as an entity separate from its owner, it must enter the name of its owner on line 3a and the owner's identifying number (social security number, or individual taxpayer identification number, or EIN) on line 3b. If the owner is a foreign person or entity and does not have a U.S. identifying number, enter "none" on line 3b. If the entity making the election is foreign, enter the name of the country in which it was formed on line 3c.

Line 4. Generally, the election will take effect on the date you enter on line 4 of this form or on the date filed if no date is entered on line 4. However, an election specifying an entity's classification for Federal tax purposes can take effect no more than 75 days prior to the date the election is filed, nor can it take effect later than 12 months after the date on which the election is filed. If line 4 shows a date more than 75 days prior to the date on which the election is filed, the election will take effect 75 days before the date it is filed. If line 4 shows an effective date more than 12 months from the filing date, the election will take effect 12 months after the date the election was filed.

Consent statement and signatures. Form 8832 must be signed by:

1. Each member of the electing entity who is an owner at the time the election is filed; or

2. Any officer, manager, or member of the electing entity who is authorized (under local law or the organizational documents) to make the election and who represents to having such authorization under penalties of perjury.

If an election is to be effective for any period prior to the time it is filed, each person who was an owner between the date the election is to be effective and the date the election is filed, and who is not an owner at the time the election is filed, must also sign.

If you need a continuation sheet or use a separate consent statement, attach it to Form 8832. The separate consent statement must contain the same information as shown on Form 8832.

Paperwork Reduction Act Notice

We ask for the information on this form to carry out the Internal Revenue laws of the United States. You are required to give us the information. We need it to ensure that you are complying with these laws and to allow us to figure and collect the right amount of tax.

You are not required to provide the information requested on a form that is subject to the Paperwork Reduction Act unless the form displays a valid OMB control number. Books or records relating to a form or its instructions must be retained as long as their contents may become material in the administration of any Internal Revenue law. Generally, tax returns and return information are confidential, as required by section 6103.

The time needed to complete and file this form will vary depending on individual circumstances. The estimated average time is:

Recordkeeping . . . 1 hr., 49 min.

Learning about the law or the form . . . 2 hr., 7 min.

Preparing and sending the form to the IRS . . . . 23 min.

If you have comments concerning the accuracy of these time estimates or suggestions for making this form simpler, we would be happy to hear from you. You can write to the Tax Forms Committee, Western Area Distribution Center, Rancho Cordova, CA 95743-0001. **Do not** send the form to this address. Instead, see **Where To File** on page 3.

Foreign Entities Classified as Corporations for Federal Tax Purposes:

American Samoa- Corporation
Argentina- Sociedad Anonima
Australia- Public Limited Company
Austria- Aktiengesellschaft
Barbados- Limited Company
Belgium- Societe Anonyme
Belize- Public Limited Company
Bolivia- Sociedad Anonima
Brazil- Sociedade Anonima
Canada- Corporation and Company
Chile- Sociedad Anonima
People's Republic of China- Gufen Youxian Gongsi
Republic of China (Taiwan)- Ku-fen Yu-hsien Kung-szu
Colombia- Sociedad Anonima
Costa Rica- Sociedad Anonima
Cyprus- Public Limited Company
Czech Republic- Akciova Spolecnost
Denmark- Aktieselskab
Ecuador- Sociedad Anonima or Compania Anonima
Egypt- Sharikat Al-Mossahamah
El Salvador- Sociedad Anonima
Finland- Julkinen Osakeyhtio/ Publikt Aktiebolag
France- Societe Anonyme
Germany- Aktiengesellschaft
Greece- Anonymos Etairia
Guam- Corporation
Guatemala- Sociedad Anonima
Guyana- Public Limited Company
Honduras- Sociedad Anonima
Hong Kong- Public Limited Company
Hungary- Reszvenytarsasag

Iceland- Hlutafelag
India- Public Limited Company
Indonesia- Perseroan Terbuka
Ireland- Public Limited Company
Israel- Public Limited Company
Italy- Societa per Azioni
Jamaica- Public Limited Company
Japan- Kabushiki Kaisha
Kazakstan- Ashyk Aktsionerlik Kogham
Republic of Korea- Chusik Hoesa
Liberia- Corporation
Luxembourg- Societe Anonyme
Malaysia- Berhad
Malta- Public Limited Company
Mexico- Sociedad Anonima
Morocco- Societe Anonyme
Netherlands- Naamloze Vennootschap
New Zealand- Limited Company
Nicaragua- Compania Anonima
Nigeria- Public Limited Company
Northern Mariana Islands- Corporation
Norway- Allment Aksjeselskap
Pakistan- Public Limited Company
Panama- Sociedad Anonima
Paraguay- Sociedad Anonima
Peru- Sociedad Anonima
Philippines- Stock Corporation
Poland- Spolka Akcyjna
Portugal- Sociedade Anonima
Puerto Rico- Corporation
Romania- Societe pe Actiuni
Russia- Otkrytoye Aktsionernoy Obshchestvo

Saudi Arabia- Sharikat Al-Mossahamah
Singapore- Public Limited Company
Slovak Republic- Akciova Spolocnost
South Africa- Public Limited Company
Spain- Sociedad Anonima
Surinam- Naamloze Vennootschap
Sweden- Publika Aktiebolag
Switzerland- Aktiengesellschaft
Thailand- Borisat Chamkad (Mahachon)
Trinidad and Tobago- Limited Company
Tunisia- Societe Anonyme
Turkey- Anonim Sirket
Ukraine- Aktsionerne Tovaristvo Vidkritogo Tipu
United Kingdom- Public Limited Company
United States Virgin Islands- Corporation
Uruguay- Sociedad Anonima
Venezuela- Sociedad Anonima or Compania Anonima

 See Regulations section 301.7701-2(b)(8) for any exceptions and inclusions to items on this list and for any revisions made to this list since these instructions were printed.

Bill of Sale

The undersigned, in consideration of membership interest in _____, a _____ limited liability company, hereby grants, bargains, sells, transfers and delivers unto said corporation the following goods and chattels:

To have and to hold the same forever.

And the undersigned, their heirs, successors and administrators, covenant and warrant that they are the lawful owners of the said goods and chattels and that they are free from all encumbrances. That the undersigned have the right to sell this property and that they will warrant and defend the sale of said property against the lawful claims and demands of all persons. IN WITNESS whereof the undersigned have executed this Bill of Sale this ____ day of _____, _____.

_____

_____

_____

This page intentionally left blank.

Limited Liability Company
Member-Managed Operating Agreement of

_____

THIS AGREEMENT is made effective as of _____, _____ among the member(s) and the company.

1. Formation. A limited liability company of the above name has been formed under the laws of the state of _____ by filing articles of organization with the secretary of state. The purpose of the business shall be to carry on any activity which is lawful under the jurisdiction in which it operates. The company may operate under a fictitious name or names as long as the company is in compliance with applicable fictitious name registration laws. The term of the company shall be perpetual or until dissolved as provided by law or by vote of the member(s) as provided in this agreement. Upon dissolution the remaining members shall have the power to continue the operation of the company as long as necessary and allowable under state law until the winding up of the affairs of the business has been completed.

2. Members. The initial member(s) shall be listed on Schedule A, which shall accompany and be made a part of this agreement. Additional members may be admitted to membership upon the unanimous consent of the current members. Transfer or pledge of a member's interest may not be made except upon consent of all members.

3. Contributions. The initial capital contribution(s) shall be listed on Schedule A. No member shall be obligated to contribute any more than the amount set forth on Schedule A unless agreed to in writing by all of the members and no member shall have any personal liability for any debt, obligation or liability of the company other than for full payment of his or her capital contribution. No member shall be entitled to interest on the capital contribution. Member voting rights shall be in proportion to the amount of their contributions.

4. Profit and Loss. The profits and losses of the business, and all other taxable or deductible items shall be allocated to the members according to the percentages on Schedule A. Distributions of profits can be made to the member(s) at any time and in any amount, except where prohibited by law.

5. Distributions. The company shall have the power to make distributions to its members in such amounts and at such intervals as a majority of the members deem appropriate according to law.

6. Management. The limited liability company shall be managed by its members listed on schedule A, which shall accompany and be made a part of this agreement. Any member may bind the company in all matters in the ordinary course of company business. In the event of a dispute between members, final determination shall be made with a vote by the members, votes being proportioned according to capital contributions.

7. Registered Agent. The company shall at all times have a registered agent and registered office. The initial registered agent and registered office shall be listed on Schedule A.

8. Assets. The assets of the company shall be registered in the legal name of the company and not in the names of the individual members.

9. Records and Accounting. The company shall keep an accurate accounting of its affairs using any method of accounting allowed by law. All members shall have a right to inspect the records during normal business hours. The members shall have the power to hire such accountants as they deem necessary or desirable.

10. Banking. The members of the company shall be authorized to set up bank accounts as in their sole discretion are deemed necessary and are authorized to execute any banking resolutions provided by the institution in which the accounts are being set up.

11. Taxes. The company shall file such tax returns as required by law. The company shall elect to be taxed as a majority of the members decide is in their best interests. The "tax matters partner," as required by the Internal Revenue Code, shall be listed on Schedule A.

12. Separate Entity. The company is a legal entity separate from its members. No member shall have any separate liability for any debts, obligations or liability of the company except as provided in this agreement.

13. Indemnity and Exculpation. The limited liability company shall indemnify and hold harmless its members, managers, employees and agents to the fullest extent allowed by law for acts or omissions done as part of their duties to or for the company. Indemnification shall include all liabilities, expenses, attorney and accountant fees, and other costs reasonably expended. No member shall be liable to the company for acts done in good faith.

14. Meetings. The members shall have no obligation to hold annual or any other meeting, but may hold such meetings if they deem them necessary or desirable.

15. Amendment of this Agreement. This agreement may not be amended except in writing signed by all of the members.

16. Conflict of interest. No member shall be involved with any business or undertaking which competes with the interests of the company except upon agreement in writing by all of the members.

17. Deadlock. In the event that the members cannot come to an agreement on any matter the members agree to submit the issue to mediation to be paid for by the company. In the event the mediation is unsuccessful, they agree to seek arbitration under the rules of the American Arbitration Association.

18. Dissociation of a member. A member shall have the right to discontinue membership upon giving thirty days notice. A member shall cease to have the right to membership upon death, court-ordered incapacity, bankruptcy or expulsion. The company shall have the right to buy the interest of any dissociated member at fair market value.

19. Dissolution. The company shall dissolve upon the unanimous consent of all the members or upon any event requiring dissolution under state law. In the event of the death, bankruptcy, permanent incapacity, or withdrawal of a member the remaining members may elect to dissolve or to continue the operation of the company.

20. General Provisions. This agreement is intended to represent the entire agreement between the parties. In the event that any party of this agreement is held to be contrary to law or unenforceable, said party shall be considered amended to comply with the law and such holding shall not affect the enforceability of other terms of this agreement. This agreement shall be binding upon the heirs, successors and assigns of the members.

21. Miscellaneous. _____
_____
_____
_____
_____
_____
_____

IN WITNESS whereof, the members of the limited liability company sign this agreement and adopt it as their operating agreement this _____ day of _____, _____.

_____   _____

_____   _____

_____   _____

Limited Liability Company
Management Operating Agreement of

_____

THIS AGREEMENT is made effective as of _____, _____ among the member(s) and the company.

1. Formation. A limited liability company of the above name has been formed under the laws of the state of _____ by filing articles of organization with the secretary of state. The purpose of the business shall be to carry on any activity which is lawful under the jurisdiction in which it operates. The company may operate under a fictitious name or names as long as the company is in compliance with applicable fictitious name registration laws. The term of the company shall be perpetual or until dissolved as provided by law or by vote of the member(s) as provided in this agreement. Upon dissolution the remaining members shall have the power to continue the operation of the company as long as necessary and allowable under state law until the winding up of the affairs of the business has been completed.

2. Members. The initial member(s) shall be listed on Schedule A, which shall accompany and be made a part of this agreement. Additional members may be admitted to membership upon the unanimous consent of the current members. Transfer or pledge of a member's interest may not be made except upon consent of all members.

3. Contributions. The initial capital contribution(s) shall be listed on Schedule A. No member shall be obligated to contribute any more than the amount set forth on Schedule A unless agreed to in writing by all of the members. No member shall have any personal liability for any debt, obligation or liability of the company other than for full payment of his or her capital contribution. No member shall be entitled to interest on the capital contribution. Member voting rights shall be in proportion to the amount of their contributions.

4. Profit and Loss. The profits and losses of the business, and all other taxable or deductible items shall be allocated to the members according to the percentages on Schedule A. Distributions of profits can be made to the member(s) at any time and in any amount, except where prohibited by law.

5. Distributions. The company shall have the power to make distributions to its members in such amounts and at such intervals as a majority of the members deem appropriate according to law.

6. Management. The limited liability company shall be managed by the managers listed on schedule A. Any manager may bind the company in all matters in the ordinary course of company business. These managers may or may not be members of the company and each manager shall have an equal vote with other managers as to management decisions. Managers shall serve until resignation or death or until they are removed by a majority vote of the members. Replacement managers shall be selected by a majority vote of the members. Managers shall have no personal liability for expenses, obligations or liabilities of the company.

7. Registered Agent. The company shall at all times have a registered agent and registered office. The initial registered agent and registered office shall be listed on Schedule A.

8. Assets. The assets of the company shall be registered in the legal name of the company and not in the names of the individual members.

9. Records and Accounting. The company shall keep an accurate accounting of its affairs using any method of accounting allowed by law. All members shall have a right to inspect the records during normal business hours. The members shall have the power to hire such accountants as they deem necessary or desirable.

10. Banking. The members of the company shall be authorized to set up bank accounts as in their sole discretion are deemed necessary and are authorized to execute any banking resolutions provided by the institution in which the accounts are being set up.

11. Taxes. The company shall file such tax returns as required by law. The company shall elect to be taxed as a majority of the members decide is in their best interests. The "tax matters partner," as required by the Internal Revenue Code, shall be listed on Schedule A.

12. Separate Entity. The company is a legal entity separate from its members. No member shall have any separate liability for any debts, obligations or liability of the company except as provided in this agreement.

13. Indemnity and Exculpation. The limited liability company shall indemnify and hold harmless its members, managers, employees and agents to the fullest extent allowed by law for acts or omissions done as part of their duties to or for the company. Indemnification shall include all liabilities, expenses, attorney and accountant fees, and other costs reasonably expended. No member shall be liable to the company for acts done in good faith.

14. Meetings. The members shall have no obligation to hold annual or any other meeting, but may hold such meetings if they deem them necessary or desirable.

15. Amendment of this Agreement. This agreement may not be amended except in writing signed by all of the members.

16. Conflict of interest. No member shall be involved with any business or undertaking which competes with the interests of the company except upon agreement in writing by all of the members.

17. Deadlock. In the event that the members cannot come to an agreement on any matter the members agree to submit the issue to mediation to be paid for by the company. In the event the mediation is unsuccessful, they agree to seek arbitration under the rules of the American Arbitration Association.

18. Dissociation of a member. A member shall have the right to discontinue membership upon giving thirty days notice. A member shall cease to have the right to membership upon death, court-ordered incapacity, bankruptcy or expulsion. The company shall have the right to buy the interest of any dissociated member at fair market value.

19. Dissolution. The company shall dissolve upon the unanimous consent of all the members or upon any event requiring dissolution under state law. In the event of the death, bankruptcy, permanent incapacity, or withdrawal of a member the remaining members may elect to dissolve or to continue the operation of the company.

20. General Provisions. This agreement is intended to represent the entire agreement between the parties. In the event that any party of this agreement is held to be contrary to law or unenforceable, said party shall be considered amended to comply with the law and such holding shall not affect the enforceability of other terms of this agreement. This agreement shall be binding upon the heirs, successors and assigns of the members.

21. Miscellaneous. _____

_____

_____

_____

_____

_____

IN WITNESS whereof, the members of the limited liability company sign this agreement and adopt it as their operating agreement this _____ day of _____, _____.

_____   _____

_____   _____

_____   _____

Schedule A to
Limited Liability Company
Operating or Management Agreement of

_____

1. Initial member(s): The initial member(s) are:

2. Capital contribution(s): The capital contribution(s) of the member(s) is/are:

3. Profits and losses: The profits, losses and other tax matters shall be allocated among the members in the following percentages:

4. Management. The company shall be managed by:

5. Registered Agent: the initial registered agent and registered office of the company are:

6. The tax matters partner is:

This page intentionally left blank.

Minutes of a Meeting of Members of

_____

A meeting of the members of the company was held on _____, at
_____.

The following were present, being all the members of the limited liability company:

_____   _____
_____   _____
_____   _____

The meeting was called to order and it was moved, seconded and unanimously carried that
_____ act as Chairman and that _____ act
as Secretary.

After discussion and upon motion duly made, seconded and carried the following resolution(s)
were adopted:

There being no further business to come before the meeting, upon motion duly made,
seconded and unanimously carried, it was adjourned.

_____
Secretary

Members:

_____

_____

_____

This page intentionally left blank.

Certificate of Authority

for

_____

This is to certify that the above Limited Liability Company is managed by its

❏ members

❏ managers

who are listed below and that each of them is authorized and empowered to transact business on behalf of the company.

Name

Address

_____   _____

_____   _____

_____

_____   _____

_____   _____

Date: _____

Name of company:

_____

By: _____

Position: _____

This page intentionally left blank.

Banking Resolution of

_____

    The undersigned, being a member of the above limited liability company authorized to sign this resolution, hereby certifies that on the _____ day of _____, _____ the members of the limited liability company adopted the following resolution:

    RESOLVED that the limited liability company open bank accounts with _____ and that the members of the company are authorized to take such action as is necessary to open such accounts; that the bank's printed form of resolution is hereby adopted and incorporated into these minutes by reference; that any ____ of the following person(s) shall have signature authority over the account:

_____   _____

_____   _____

and that said resolution has not been modified or rescinded.

Date: _____

                             _____
                             Authorized member

This page intentionally left blank.

Resolution
of

_____

a Limited Liability Company

RESOLVED that the company elects to be taxed as follows:

❏ a single member electing to disregard the separate entity
❏ a multiple member entity electing to be taxed as a partnership
❏ a multiple member entity electing to be taxed as a corporation

for tax purposes under the Internal Revenue Code and that the managers or managing members of the limited liability company are directed to file IRS Form 8832 and to take any further action necessary for the company to qualify for said tax status.

Members' Consent

The undersigned shareholders being all of the members of the above limited liability company hereby consent to the above tax election.

Date:_____

Name of member	Percentage owned	Signature
_____	_____	_____
_____	_____	_____
_____	_____	_____
_____	_____	_____

This page intentionally left blank.

Certificate of Amendment
to
Articles of Organization
of

_____

a Limited Liability Company

First: The date of filing of the original Articles of Organization was: _____

Second: The following amendment(s) to the Articles of Organization was/were duly adopted by the limited liability company:

Date: _____

_____

_____

This page intentionally left blank.

Change of Registered Agent and/or Registered Office

1.   The name of the limited liability company is:

2.   The street address of the current registered office is:

3.   The new address of the registered office is to be:

4.   The current registered agent is:

5.   The new registered agent is:

6.   The street address of the registered office and the street address of the business address of the registered agent are identical.

7.   Such change was duly authorized by the members of the limited liability company.

_____

Having been named as registered agent and to accept service of process for the above stated limited liability company at the place designated in this certificate, I hereby accept the appointment as registered agent and agree to act in this capacity. I further agree to comply with the provisions of all statutes relating to the proper and complete performance of my duties, and am familiar with and accept the obligations of my position as registered agent.

_____
Registered Agent

INDEX

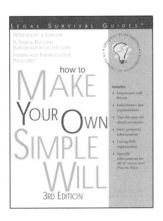

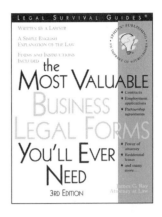

SPHINX® PUBLISHING'S NATIONAL TITLES

Valid in All 50 States

LEGAL SURVIVAL IN BUSINESS

The Complete Book of Corporate Forms	$24.95
The Complete Patent Book	$26.95
The Entrepreneur's Internet Handbook	$21.95
How to Form a Limited Liability Company (2E)	$24.95
Incorporate in Delaware from Any State	$24.95
Incorporate in Nevada from Any State	$24.95
How to Form a Nonprofit Corporation (2E)	$24.95
How to Form Your Own Corporation (3E)	$24.95
How to Form Your Own Partnership (2E)	$24.95
How to Register Your Own Copyright (4E)	$24.95
How to Register Your Own Trademark (3E)	$21.95
Most Valuable Business Legal Forms You'll Ever Need (3E)	$21.95
The Small Business Owner's Guide to Bankruptcy	$21.95

LEGAL SURVIVAL IN COURT

Crime Victim's Guide to Justice (2E)	$21.95
Grandparents' Rights (3E)	$24.95
Help Your Lawyer Win Your Case (2E)	$14.95
Jurors' Rights (2E)	$12.95
Legal Research Made Easy (3E)	$21.95
Winning Your Personal Injury Claim (2E)	$24.95
Your Rights When You Owe Too Much	$16.95

LEGAL SURVIVAL IN REAL ESTATE

Essential Guide to Real Estate Contracts	$18.95
Essential Guide to Real Estate Leases	$18.95
How to Buy a Condominium or Townhome (2E)	$19.95

LEGAL SURVIVAL IN PERSONAL AFFAIRS

Cómo Hacer su Propio Testamento	$16.95
Cómo Solicitar su Propio Divorcio	$24.95
Cómo Restablecer su propio Crédito y Renegociar sus Deudas	$21.95
Family Limited Partnership	$26.95
Guía de Inmigración a Estados Unidos (3E)	$24.95
Guía de Justicia para Víctimas del Crimen	$21.95
The 529 College Savings Plan	$16.95
The Complete Legal Guide to Senior Care	$21.95
How to File Your Own Bankruptcy (5E)	$21.95
How to File Your Own Divorce (4E)	$24.95
How to Make Your Own Simple Will (3E)	$18.95
How to Write Your Own Living Will (3E)	$18.95
How to Write Your Own Premarital Agreement (3E)	$24.95
Inmigración a los EE. UU. Paso a Paso	$22.95
Living Trusts and Other Ways to Avoid Probate (3E)	$24.95
Manual de Beneficios para el Seguro Social	$18.95
Mastering the MBE	$16.95
Most Valuable Personal Legal Forms You'll Ever Need	$24.95
Neighbor v. Neighbor (2E)	$16.95
The Nanny and Domestic Help Legal Kit	$22.95
The Power of Attorney Handbook (4E)	$19.95
Repair Your Own Credit and Deal with Debt	$18.95
The Social Security Benefits Handbook (3E)	$18.95
Social Security Q&A	$12.95
Sexual Harassment:Your Guide to Legal Action	$18.95
Teen Rights	$22.95
Unmarried Parents' Rights (2E)	$19.95
U.S. Immigration Step by Step	$21.95
U.S.A. Immigration Guide (4E)	$24.95
The Visitation Handbook	$18.95
Win Your Unemployment Compensation Claim (2E)	$21.95
Your Right to Child Custody, Visitation and Support (2E)	$24.95

Legal Survival Guides are directly available from Sourcebooks, Inc., or from your local bookstores.
Prices are subject to change without notice.

For credit card orders call 1–800–432–7444, write P.O. Box 4410, Naperville, IL 60567-4410
or fax 630-961-2168

SPHINX® PUBLISHING ORDER FORM

BILL TO:

SHIP TO:

Phone #

Terms

F.O.B. Chicago, IL

Ship Date

Charge my: ☐ VISA ☐ MasterCard ☐ American Express

☐ Money Order or Personal Check

Credit Card Number

Expiration Date

Qty	ISBN	Title	Retail	Ext.
		SPHINX PUBLISHING NATIONAL TITLES		
	1-57248-148-X	Cómo Hacer su Propio Testamento	$16.95	
	1-57248-226-5	Cómo Restablecer su propio Crédito y Renegociar sus Deudas	$21.95	
	1-57248-147-1	Cómo Solicitar su Propio Divorcio	$24.95	
	1-57248-238-9	The 529 College Savings Plan	$16.95	
	1-57248-166-8	The Complete Book of Corporate Forms	$24.95	
	1-57248-229-X	The Complete Legal Guide to Senior Care	$21.95	
	1-57248-201-X	The Complete Patent Book	$26.95	
	1-57248-163-3	Crime Victim's Guide to Justice (2E)	$21.95	
	1-57248-251-6	The Entrepreneur's Internet Handbook	$21.95	
	1-57248-159-5	Essential Guide to Real Estate Contracts	$18.95	
	1-57248-160-9	Essential Guide to Real Estate Leases	$18.95	
	1-57248-254-0	Family Limited Partnership	$26.95	
	1-57248-139-0	Grandparents' Rights (3E)	$24.95	
	1-57248-188-9	Guía de Inmigración a Estados Unidos (3E)	$24.95	
	1-57248-187-0	Guía de Justicia para Víctimas del Crimen	$21.95	
	1-57248-103-X	Help Your Lawyer Win Your Case (2E)	$14.95	
	1-57248-164-1	How to Buy a Condominium or Townhome (2E)	$19.95	
	1-57248-191-9	How to File Your Own Bankruptcy (5E)	$21.95	
	1-57248-132-3	How to File Your Own Divorce (4E)	$24.95	
	1-57248-222-2	How to Form a Limited Liability Company (2E)	$24.95	
	1-57248-231-1	How to Form a Nonprofit Corporation (2E)	$24.95	
	1-57248-133-1	How to Form Your Own Corporation (3E)	$24.95	
	1-57248-224-9	How to Form Your Own Partnership (2E)	$24.95	
	1-57248-232-X	How to Make Your Own Simple Will (3E)	$18.95	
	1-57248-200-1	How to Register Your Own Copyright (4E)	$24.95	
	1-57248-104-8	How to Register Your Own Trademark (3E)	$21.95	
	1-57248-233-8	How to Write Your Own Living Will (3E)	$18.95	
	1-57248-156-0	How to Write Your Own Premarital Agreement (3E)	$24.95	
	1-57248-230-3	Incorporate in Delaware from Any State	$24.95	
	1-57248-158-7	Incorporate in Nevada from Any State	$24.95	
	1-57248-250-8	Inmigración a los EE.UU. Paso a Paso	$22.95	
	1-57071-333-2	Jurors' Rights (2E)	$12.95	
	1-57248-223-0	Legal Research Made Easy (3E)	$21.95	
	1-57248-165-X	Living Trusts and Other Ways to Avoid Probate (3E)	$24.95	

Qty	ISBN	Title	Retail	Ext.
	1-57248-186-2	Manual de Beneficios para el Seguro Social	$18.95	
	1-57248-220-6	Mastering the MBE	$16.95	
	1-57248-167-6	Most Valuable Bus. Legal Forms You'll Ever Need (3E)	$21.95	
	1-57248-130-7	Most Valuable Personal Legal Forms You'll Ever Need	$24.95	
	1-57248-098-X	The Nanny and Domestic Help Legal Kit	$22.95	
	1-57248-089-0	Neighbor v. Neighbor (2E)	$16.95	
	1-57248-169-2	The Power of Attorney Handbook (4E)	$19.95	
	1-57248-149-8	Repair Your Own Credit and Deal with Debt	$18.95	
	1-57248-217-2	Sexual Harassment: Your Guide to Legal Action	$18.95	
	1-57248-219-2	The Small Business Owner's Guide to Bankruptcy	$21.95	
	1-57248-168-4	The Social Security Benefits Handbook (3E)	$18.95	
	1-57248-216-8	Social Security Q&A	$12.95	
	1-57248-221-4	Teen Rights	$22.95	
	1-57248-236-2	Unmarried Parents' Rights (2E)	$19.95	
	1-57248-161-7	U.S.A. Immigration Guide (4E)	$24.95	
	1-57248-192-7	The Visitation Handbook	$18.95	
	1-57248-225-7	Win Your Unemployment Compensation Claim (2E)	$21.95	
	1-57248-138-2	Winning Your Personal Injury Claim (2E)	$24.95	
	1-57248-162-5	Your Right to Child Custody, Visitation and Support (2E)	$24.95	
	1-57248-157-9	Your Rights When You Owe Too Much	$16.95	
		CALIFORNIA TITLES		
	1-57248-150-1	CA Power of Attorney Handbook (2E)	$18.95	
	1-57248-151-X	How to File for Divorce in CA (3E)	$26.95	
	1-57248-145-5	How to Probate and Settle an Estate in California	$26.95	
	1-57248-146-3	How to Start a Business in CA	$18.95	
	1-57248-194-3	How to Win in Small Claims Court in CA (2E)	$18.95	
	1-57248-246-X	Make Your Own CA Will	$18.95	
	1-57248-196-X	The Landlord's Legal Guide in CA	$24.95	
	1-57248-241-9	Tenants' Rights in CA	$21.95	
		FLORIDA TITLES		
	1-57071-363-4	Florida Power of Attorney Handbook (2E)	$16.95	
	1-57248-176-5	How to File for Divorce in FL (7E)	$26.95	
	1-57248-177-3	How to Form a Corporation in FL (5E)	$24.95	
	1-57248-203-6	How to Form a Limited Liability Co. in FL (2E)	$24.95	
	1-57071-401-0	How to Form a Partnership in FL	$22.95	

Form Continued on Following Page   **SUBTOTAL**

To order, call Sourcebooks at 1-800-432-7444 or FAX (630) 961-2168 (Bookstores, libraries, wholesalers—please call for discount)

Prices are subject to change without notice.

Find more legal information at: www.SphinxLegal.com

SPHINX® PUBLISHING ORDER FORM

Qty	ISBN	Title	Retail	Ext.
_____	1-57248-113-7	How to Make a FL Will (6E)	$16.95	_____
_____	1-57248-088-2	How to Modify Your FL Divorce Judgment (4E)	$24.95	_____
_____	1-57248-144-7	How to Probate and Settle an Estate in FL (4E)	$26.95	_____
_____	1-57248-081-5	How to Start a Business in FL (5E)	$16.95	_____
_____	1-57248-204-4	How to Win in Small Claims Court in FL (7E)	$18.95	_____
_____	1-57248-202-8	Land Trusts in Florida (6E)	$29.95	_____
_____	1-57248-123-4	Landlords' Rights and Duties in FL (8E)	$21.95	_____

GEORGIA TITLES

Qty	ISBN	Title	Retail	Ext.
_____	1-57248-137-4	How to File for Divorce in GA (4E)	$21.95	_____
_____	1-57248-180-3	How to Make a GA Will (4E)	$21.95	_____
_____	1-57248-140-4	How to Start a Business in Georgia (2E)	$16.95	_____

ILLINOIS TITLES

Qty	ISBN	Title	Retail	Ext.
_____	1-57248-244-3	Child Custody, Visitation, and Support in IL	$24.95	_____
_____	1-57248-206-0	How to File for Divorce in IL (3E)	$24.95	_____
_____	1-57248-170-6	How to Make an IL Will (3E)	$16.95	_____
_____	1-57248-247-8	How to Start a Business in IL (3E)	$21.95	_____
_____	1-57248-252-4	The Landlord's Legal Guide in IL	$24.95	_____

MASSACHUSETTS TITLES

Qty	ISBN	Title	Retail	Ext.
_____	1-57248-128-5	How to File for Divorce in MA (3E)	$24.95	_____
_____	1-57248-115-3	How to Form a Corporation in MA	$24.95	_____
_____	1-57248-108-0	How to Make a MA Will (2E)	$16.95	_____
_____	1-57248-248-6	How to Start a Business in MA (3E)	$21.95	_____
_____	1-57248-209-5	The Landlord's Legal Guide in MA	$24.95	_____

MICHIGAN TITLES

Qty	ISBN	Title	Retail	Ext.
_____	1-57248-215-X	How to File for Divorce in MI (3E)	$24.95	_____
_____	1-57248-182-X	How to Make a MI Will (3E)	$16.95	_____
_____	1-57248-183-8	How to Start a Business in MI (3E)	$18.95	_____

MINNESOTA TITLES

Qty	ISBN	Title	Retail	Ext.
_____	1-57248-142-0	How to File for Divorce in MN	$21.95	_____
_____	1-57248-179-X	How to Form a Corporation in MN	$24.95	_____
_____	1-57248-178-1	How to Make a MN Will (2E)	$16.95	_____

NEW YORK TITLES

Qty	ISBN	Title	Retail	Ext.
_____	1-57248-193-5	Child Custody, Visitation and Support in NY	$26.95	_____
_____	1-57248-141-2	How to File for Divorce in NY (2E)	$26.95	_____
_____	1-57248-249-4	How to Form a Corporation in NY (2E)	$24.95	_____
_____	1-57248-095-5	How to Make a NY Will (2E)	$16.95	_____
_____	1-57248-199-4	How to Start a Business in NY (2E)	$18.95	_____

Qty	ISBN	Title	Retail	Ext.
_____	1-57248-198-6	How to Win in Small Claims Court in NY (2E)	$18.95	_____
_____	1-57248-197-8	Landlords' Legal Guide in NY	$24.95	_____
_____	1-57071-188-7	New York Power of Attorney Handbook	$19.95	_____
_____	1-57248-122-6	Tenants' Rights in NY	$21.95	_____

NEW JERSEY TITLES

Qty	ISBN	Title	Retail	Ext.
_____	1-57248-239-7	How to File for Divorce in NJ	$24.95	_____

NORTH CAROLINA TITLES

Qty	ISBN	Title	Retail	Ext.
_____	1-57248-185-4	How to File for Divorce in NC (3E)	$22.95	_____
_____	1-57248-129-3	How to Make a NC Will (3E)	$16.95	_____
_____	1-57248-184-6	How to Start a Business in NC (3E)	$18.95	_____
_____	1-57248-091-2	Landlords' Rights & Duties in NC	$21.95	_____

OHIO TITLES

Qty	ISBN	Title	Retail	Ext.
_____	1-57248-190-0	How to File for Divorce in OH (2E)	$24.95	_____
_____	1-57248-174-9	How to Form a Corporation in OH	$24.95	_____
_____	1-57248-173-0	How to Make an OH Will	$16.95	_____

PENNSYLVANIA TITLES

Qty	ISBN	Title	Retail	Ext.
_____	1-57248-242-7	Child Custody, Visitation and Support in Pennsylvania	$26.95	_____
_____	1-57248-211-7	How to File for Divorce in PA (3E)	$26.95	_____
_____	1-57248-094-7	How to Make a PA Will (2E)	$16.95	_____
_____	1-57248-112-9	How to Start a Business in PA (2E)	$18.95	_____
_____	1-57248-245-1	The Landlord's Legal Guide in PA	$24.95	_____

TEXAS TITLES

Qty	ISBN	Title	Retail	Ext.
_____	1-57248-171-4	Child Custody, Visitation, and Support in TX	$22.95	_____
_____	1-57248-172-2	How to File for Divorce in TX (3E)	$24.95	_____
_____	1-57248-114-5	How to Form a Corporation in TX (2E)	$24.95	_____
_____	1-57248-255-9	How to Make a TX Will (3E)	$16.95	_____
_____	1-57248-214-1	How to Probate and Settle an Estate in TX (3E)	$26.95	_____
_____	1-57248-228-1	How to Start a Business in TX (3E)	$18.95	_____
_____	1-57248-111-0	How to Win in Small Claims Court in TX (2E)	$16.95	_____
_____	1-57248-110-2	Landlords' Rights and Duties in TX (2E)	$21.95	_____

SUBTOTAL THIS PAGE _____

SUBTOTAL PREVIOUS PAGE _____

Shipping — $5.00 for 1st book, $1.00 each additional _____

Illinois residents add 6.75% sales tax _____

Connecticut residents add 6.00% sales tax _____

TOTAL _____

To order, call Sourcebooks at 1-800-432-7444 or FAX (630) 961-2168 (Bookstores, libraries, wholesalers—please call for discount)
Prices are subject to change without notice.
Find more legal information at: **www.SphinxLegal.com**